GEORGE WASHINGTON & RELIGION

GEORGE WASHINGTON & RELIGION

PAUL F. BOLLER, JR.

SOUTHERN METHODIST UNIVERSITY PRESS: DALLAS

LIBRARY OF CONGRESS CATALOG CARD NUMBER: 63-9755

PRINTED IN THE UNITED STATES OF AMERICA AT DALLAS, TEXAS

TO
MY FATHER AND MOTHER

PREFACE

THE PLACE of religion in the life and thought of George Washington has long deserved careful examination. Perhaps nothing about Washington has been so thoroughly clouded by myth, legend, misunderstanding, and misrepresentation as his religious outlook. Literature on the subject (as on every other aspect of his life) has, of course, been voluminous. Since the early nineteenth century hundreds of books, pamphlets, articles, sermons, orations, and essays discussing Washington's religion have been published. Few of them, however, have been characterized by the spirit of detachment, and none of them by the comprehensiveness of scope needed to enable us to understand with precision and in depth what Washington's religious opinions were and how they affected his attitude toward religious freedom, the rights of conscience, and the relations between church and state in the young American nation.

Students of American intellectual history, for obvious reasons, have not, in the main, regarded Washington as a fruitful subject of inquiry. He was not, after all, an "intellectual" in the sense that Benjamin Franklin, Thomas Jefferson, Thomas Paine, and John Adams can be considered "intellectuals." Still, the very fact that Washington never articulated his views in an orderly fashion, as Franklin, Jefferson, Paine, and Adams did from time to time, makes the investigation of his opinions all the more challenging. Washington did have definite opinions on religion and he expressed them,

in passing, on numerous occasions. It is worth finding out
what they were. Though primarily a man of action, Washington, with his enormous moral prestige, had an undoubted
effect on the thought of the new nation. His views are at
least as pertinent to an understanding of ideas in America
as those of, say, Andrew Jackson, who has been a favorite
with students of intellectual history.

When it comes to Washington's religion, professional
historians and biographers writing in the twentieth century
have tended either to pass over the subject in silence, to
classify Washington with Franklin, Jefferson, and Paine, and
then pass on to another topic, or to describe only the more
obvious aspects of Washington's religious behavior. The field
has thus been left largely to writers with *parti pris*. Historians
with sectarian attachments have been eager to emphasize—
and they inevitably exaggerate—the extent of Washington's
associations with and partiality for their particular denominations. Evangelical writers and filiopietists have busily accumulated pious fables about Washington's religious habits
whose historicity many Americans today still regard as
unquestioned. Militant secularists, on the other hand, have
been so preoccupied with the useful and necessary work
of exploding the myths about Washington that they have
had neither the time nor the inclination to inquire into the
actualities of Washington's religious life. Their uniform
assumption, however, is that whatever Washington may
have said in public, he was, at heart, an anticlerical.

The tendency of writers to portray Washington, religiously, in their own image reminds one of the little boy
in Professor Thomas Gallaudet's school for deaf-mutes who
was asked whether he knew the story about Washington
and the hatchet. The little fellow said he did and began

telling it off with his fingers. When he reached the great confrontation scene in the story, he said: "And Washington took the hatchet in his left hand and he said to his father ..."At this point Professor Gallaudet interrupted to ask: "Why did he take the hatchet in his left hand?" "Because," cried the boy with some impatience, "he wanted his right hand to tell him with!" In taking it for granted that Washington was like himself, Professor Gallaudet's pupil did not differ materially from the majority of his elders who have spoken or written about Washington's religious beliefs and practices.

It is clear, then, that a full-scale, critical study of Washington's religion has been sorely needed. In what follows I have attempted to separate the myths from the facts and to make a systematic analysis of Washington's religion in all its ramifications on the basis of what may be regarded as trustworthy records: his behavior as a churchman, his attitude toward the place of organized religion in society, his position with regard to Christianity, his religious philosophy as it emerges from his private writings. Finally, I have endeavored to assess his contribution to the development of religious liberty in the United States. Throughout I have also tried to emphasize the impact of Washington's religious behavior on his contemporaries and upon later generations of Americans.

As sources I have depended largely on Washington's own writings, public and private, together with statements by his contemporaries, whose authority can be taken as reliable, on various phases of his religious life. In controversial areas —such as, for example, the question of whether Washington was a Christian or not—I have necessarily, after examining all the evidence, had to make my own judgments. That not everyone will concur in these judgments is to be expected. I do believe, however, that what I have had to say deserves serious consideration in any attempt to understand the religious opinions of George Washington.

I should like to express my warm appreciation for the interest and encouragement shown by Allen Maxwell, Margaret Hartley, and Donald Wetzel of the Southern Methodist University Press while I was writing this book and especially for the pleasure I derived from working with Margaret Hartley—despite our occasional disagreements over points of style—in preparing the manuscript for publication.

I am grateful to the following publishers for permission to quote from books to which they hold the copyright: Charles Scribner's Sons for Douglas Southall Freeman, *George Washington: A Biography*, Volume V, *Victory with the Help of France;* Dorrance and Company for Joseph Buffington, *The Soul of Washington;* the Jewish Publication Society of America for Lee M. Friedman, *Jewish Pioneers and Patriots;* and the New York Public Library for Victor Paltsits, *Washington's Farewell Address.* And I express appreciation for permission to quote a passage from *Jewish Notables in America, 1776-1865* by Harry Simonhoff, copyright 1956 by the author, reprinted by permission of Chilton Books, Philadelphia and New York.

Portions of this book have appeared in somewhat different form in the *Bulletin of Friends Historical Society, Journal of the Presbyterian Historical Society,* the *Southwest Review,* and the *William and Mary Quarterly.*

PAUL F. BOLLER, JR.

Southern Methodist University
Dallas, Texas
December 8, 1962

CONTENTS

GEORGE
WASHINGTON
& RELIGION

I

WASHINGTON
AND THE PIETISTS

"ONE PLEASANT EVENING in the month of June, in the year
17__," begins a popular tale of the early nineteenth century,

a man was observed entering the borders of a wood near the
Hudson river, his appearance that of a person above the common
rank. The inhabitants of a country village would have dignified
him with the title of squire, and from his manner, have pronounced him proud; but those more accustomed to society would
inform you, there was something like a military air about him.

Suddenly a storm came up: the lightning flashed, the
thunder pealed, and the rain pelted downward. For a time
the traveler took shelter under a large oak tree; but at length,
espying a light glimmering through the trees, he made his
way with difficulty through the mud to a nearby farmhouse.
Here he was welcomed by a farmer and his wife, provided
with food and warmth, and his horse taken care of in a
"well-stored" barn. After supper, the farmer informed the
stranger

that it was now the hour at which the family performed their evening devotions, inviting him at the same time to be present. The invitation was accepted in these words:

"It would afford me the greatest pleasure to commune with my heavenly Preserver, after the events of the day; such exercises prepare us for the repose we seek in sleep."

The host now reached his Bible from the shelf, and after reading a chapter and singing, concluded the whole with a fervent prayer; then lighting a pine-knot, conducted the person he had entertained to his chamber, wished him good night's rest and retired to the adjoining apartment.

Presently:

The sound of a voice came from the chamber of their guest, who was now engaged in his *private religious worship*. After thanking the Creator for his many mercies, and asking a blessing on the inhabitants of the house, he continued, "And now, almighty Father, if it is thy holy will, that we shall obtain a place and a name among the nations of the earth, grant that we may be enabled to show our gratitude for thy goodness, by our endeavours to fear and obey thee. Bless us with wisdom in our councils, success in battle, and let all our victories be tempered with humanity. Endow also our enemies with enlightened minds, that they may become sensible of their injustice, and willing to restore our liberty and peace. Grant the petition of thy servant for the sake of Him whom thou hast called thy beloved Son; nevertheless, not my will, but thine be done. Amen."

The following morning, the stranger thanked the good couple warmly for their hospitality and just before leaving he announced: "My name is GEORGE WASHINGTON." So goes one of the more elaborate stories about Washington's piety that began circulating in this country shortly after his death in 1799.[1]

There were many such stories. In fact, if one were to take seriously the host of books and articles filled with tales of this kind about George Washington, written by zealous filiopietists with an evangelical bent during the past 160 years, he would be tempted to conclude that the Father of his Country missed his calling: he should have been a circuit-riding evangelist. He was, according to these accounts, "a lay leader of the Episcopal church,"[2] "a Christian hero and statesman,"[3] "Christ's faithful soldier and servant,"[4] "the founder of a Christian republic,"[5] "the great high-priest of the nation";[6] and at one time it was even suggested that he be duly canonized as the first official saint of the church to which he belonged.[7]

Indeed, judging from the many instances of Washington's preoccupation with devout observances which were accumulated over the years by such enthusiasts as Mason Locke Weems, Edward C. McGuire, William Meade, William J. Johnstone, Joseph Buffington, and W. Herbert Burk, to name only the most influential, it would appear that Washington had time for little else but the ritual of piety.[8] He attended church regularly, said grace at mealtime, was active in church work, went out of his way to receive the sacrament of the Lord's Supper when away from home, filled his utterances, both official and unofficial, with religious exhortations, and observed private devotions with almost relentless regularity wherever he happened to be—in his library, in his army tent, at the homes of friends and strangers, and in woods, thickets, groves, and bushes, if no shelter was at hand.

He seems, in fact, to have been perpetually at prayer. He prayed first thing in the morning upon rising (4 or

5 A.M.) and last thing before retiring at night (9 P.M.);[9] he composed a little book of prayers entitled *The Daily Sacrifice* when he was about twenty years old;[10] he was "the gentleman who always kneels down in prayer" in the Continental Congress;[11] he "wrestled in prayer with the God of battles" before each Revolutionary encounter with the enemy;[12] he composed a prayer on the occasion of the signing of the Declaration of Independence;[13] he fell to the ground, tears streaming down his face, in a prayer of thanksgiving when he heard of the victory at Saratoga;[14] and at times, when in company, "he would sit as if he forgot that he was not alone and raising his hand would move his lips evidently in prayer."[15] And Washington's prayers were by no means perfunctory invocations. In his biography of Washington, Woodrow Wilson reported that a little girl overheard Washington crying out on the eve of battle: "The Lord God of gods, the Lord God of gods, He knoweth, and Israel he shall know; if it be in rebellion, or if in transgression against the Lord (save us not this day)."[16]

People, it seems, like the girl in Wilson's story, were always stumbling upon Washington at prayer. Sometimes it was children. In her *Memoirs of Washington* (1857), Caroline M. Kirkland said that Rev. D. D. Field told her that a Mrs. Watkins told him that

when she was a girl, General Washington lived four months at her father's during the Revolution, and that she had been by the side of his room and heard him at prayer.... She said that his room was in a distant part of the building, and that she had to pass through several rooms to get by the side of the general's room. She stated that her sisters used to go with her and listen, and that their father, learning what they were doing, checked them for it.[17]

Sometimes it was youthful members of Washington's own household. B. F. Morris had it from Nathan Hewitt, who had it from a Rev. Mr. Wilson, that a nephew of Washington's, curious about what his uncle did in the library between nine and ten o'clock every evening, decided to do a little eavesdropping. Accordingly:

During a violent storm of wind and rain, and when there were no visitors, he crept in his stocking-feet to the door, and through the key-hole he beheld him *on his knees,* with a large book open before him, which he had no doubt was a Bible,—a large one being constantly in the room.[18]

More frequently, however, it was army officers who listened in on Washington's private devotions. According to T. W. J. Wylie,

One of the officers of his bodyguard mentions, that once despatches were received about daybreak, which he was to communicate at once to the Commander-in-chief. On passing through a narrow entry to his apartment, he heard a suppressed and earnest voice; and, on passing, he found that General Washington was engaged in prayer. Another officer says, that on a sudden entrance into his tent, he had repeatedly found him on his knees.[19]

And John F. Watson related that Joseph Eastburn told Richard Loxley that once, while he was on camp duty near Princeton,

he heard when entering a thicket, the audible utterance of some solemn voice, and seeking further for the cause, found Gen. Washington upon his knees in prayer. He retired hastily, fully satisfied in his own conviction, that he was a great man who feared God and *trusted* in his worship.[20]

On at least one occasion, Washington is said to have reacted violently to this almost daily (one gathers) intrusion upon his privacy. One day at Valley Forge, the story goes, Washington retired to his quarters after giving his orderly strict instructions not to admit anyone under any circumstances whatsoever. Suddenly, while the orderly was listening in fascination to the "low murmurs" of prayer emanating from Washington's tent, an officer approached with urgent news for the American commander. The orderly tried to bar his way, but the officer pushed him aside and knocked impatiently on the tent pole. Immediately, Washington, without rising from his knees, turned, drew his pistol, and fired at the officer. He then put his weapon back in the holster and resumed his quiet devotions. Whether the intruder was killed, wounded, or merely frightened away, it is not given us to know.[21]

The source for many of the legends about Washington's religiosity was, of course, the irrepressible Mason Locke ("Parson") Weems, the Anglican minister and popular writer who, not long after Washington's death, published the first and unquestionably the most diverting of all the Washington biographies. The tale about little George and the cherry tree (added in the fifth edition in 1806)[22] is undoubtedly the most delightfully narrated of all Parson Weems's fanciful anecdotes about Washington. But his story about the Quaker who abandoned his pacifism after hearing Washington pray (a favorite with the pietists) is itself not without charm. "In the winter of 1777," as Weems describes the incident,

while Washington, with the American army, lay encamped at Valley Forge, a certain good old FRIEND, of the respectable family and name of Potts, if I mistake not, had occasion to pass through the woods near headquarters. Treading his way along the venerable grove, suddenly he heard the sound of a human voice, which, as he advanced, increased on his ear; and at length became like the voice of one speaking much in earnest. As he approached the spot with a cautious step, whom should he behold, in a dark natural bower of ancient oaks, but the commander in chief of the American armies on his knees in prayer! Motionless with surprise, friend Potts continued on the place till the general, having ended his devotions, arose; and, with a countenance of angelic serenity, retired to headquarters. Friend Potts then went home, and on entering his parlour called out to his wife, "Sarah! my dear Sarah! all's well! all's well! George Washington will yet prevail!"

"What's the matter, Isaac?" replied she, "thee seems moved."

"Well, if I seem moved, 'tis no more than what I really am. I have this day seen what I never expected. Thee knows that I always thought that the sword and the gospel were utterly inconsistent; and that no man could be a soldier and a christian at the same time. But George Washington has this day convinced me of my mistake."

He then related what he had seen, and concluded with this prophetical remark—"If George Washington be not a man of God, I am greatly deceived—and still more shall I be deceived, if God do not, through him, work out a great salvation for America."[23]

The Potts story has been the most cherished of all the anecdotes about Washington at prayer, though, interestingly, it was never alluded to by Quaker writers on Washington, not even by those of a "Free Quaker" or nonpacifist persuasion. It has been repeated with countless variations since Weems first put it forward; scores of witnesses attesting to the event (many years later) have been dug up by champions of the story; and many details have been added by later writers to Weems's original account. Isaac Potts, according to later versions of the event, was a Quaker preacher; he saw "the tears flowing copiously" down Washington's cheeks during the prayer and he himself "burst into tears"[24] as he told his wife (variously referred to as Sarah, Betty, and Martha)[25] about his experience. In addition, good patriot that he had become, he thereafter "sent Washington many items concerning movements of the enemy."[26]

The Valley Forge story is, of course, utterly without foundation in fact. There was indeed a Quaker farmer named Isaac Potts who came into possession of a house in Valley Forge toward the end of the Revolutionary War; but he was nowhere near Valley Forge in the winter of 1777 when Washington was supposed to have been praying in the snow.[27] Nevertheless, Washington's "Gethsemane,"[28] as the Valley Forge episode has been called, was eventually fixed in bronze on the Sub-Treasury Building in New York City and Potts's house itself was made into a shrine.[29] It has also been celebrated in verse:

> Oh! who shall know the might
> Of the words he utter'd there?
> The fate of nations there was turn'd
> By the fervor of his prayer.
>
> But wouldst thou know his name
> Who wandered there alone?
> Go, read enrolled in Heaven's archives,
> *The prayer* of Washington![30]

In June, 1903, moreover, the cornerstone of the million-dollar Washington Memorial Chapel, commemorating the event, was laid in Valley Forge;[31] in 1928 the United States government issued a batch of two-cent stamps showing Washington praying at Valley Forge;[32] and in 1955 a private chapel for the use of United States congressmen was opened in the Capitol containing, as its chief feature, a stained-glass window above an oak altar depicting the kneeling figure of Washington at Valley Forge.[33] Even Weems, one guesses, would have been somewhat thunderstruck by the solemn literalness with which many of his readers interpreted his exuberant narrative of *The Life of George Washington; with Curious Anecdotes, Equally Honourable to Himself, and Exemplary to His Young Countrymen.*

Second only in popularity to the Valley Forge tale has been the story (which Weems somehow missed) that one Sunday morning, during the Revolution, Washington requested and received permission to attend a communion service held by the Presbyterian church in Morristown, New Jersey. The Morristown story was first advanced by Rev. Samuel H. Cox, pastor of the Laight Street Presbyterian Church in New York City. In a letter to David Hosack dated March 20, 1828, which the latter included, somewhat irrelevantly, in a footnote in his *Memoir of DeWitt Clinton*, published the following year, Mr. Cox said:

While the American army, under the command of Washington, lay encamped in the environs of Morris Town, New-Jersey, it occurred that the service of the communion . . . was to be administered in the Presbyterian church of that village. In a morning of the previous week, the General, after his accustomed inspection of the camp, visited the house of Rev. Dr. Jones, then pastor of that church, and after the usual preliminaries, thus accosted him. "Doctor, I understand that the Lord's Supper is to be celebrated with you next Sunday; I would learn if it accords with the canons of your church to admit communicants of another denomination?" The Doctor rejoined—"Most certainly; ours is not the Presbyterian table, General, but the Lord's table; and hence we give the Lord's invitation to all of his followers, of whatever name." The General replied, "I am glad of it; that is as it ought to be; but as I was not quite sure of the fact, I thought I would ascertain it from yourself, as I propose to join with you on that occasion. Though a member of the Church of England, I have no exclusive partialities." The Doctor re-assured him of a cordial welcome, and the General was found seated with the communicants the next Sabbath.[34]

The anecdote seems to have attracted little or no attention until Rev. Edward G. McGuire included it in *The Religious Opinions and Character of Washington* eight years later, identified the clergyman who administered the sacrament as Rev. Timothy Johnes, and presented the results of his efforts to locate evidence to corroborate Cox's story. It was impossible, McGuire discovered, to find any living witness to the event; moreover, William Johnes, son of Timothy, could "say nothing on the subject" because of his "great age"; William's wife, however, who was much younger, insisted that it was an "unquestioned family tradition" and older residents of Morristown also regarded the occurrence as "certain."[35] Furthermore, Dr. James Richards of Auburn Theological Seminary, who had served in the Morristown church some years after Timothy Johnes' pastorate, assured McGuire that the story about Washington was "universally current" while he was living in Morristown and, "as far as I know, never contradicted."[36] During the course of his investigations, McGuire heard that Washington made his request in writing rather than in person and that Dr. Richards was in possession of the Washington note. But Dr. Richards, he learned to his disappointment, did not possess the note nor had he ever seen it; nevertheless, he assured McGuire that he had no doubt "that such a note was addressed by Washington to Dr. Johnes, of Morristown, on the occasion to which you refer." McGuire accepted Dr. Richards' assurances as conclusive.[37]

After McGuire, a host of writers (not all of them by any means Presbyterian) picked up the story, added colorful details to it, and collected additional statements by descendants of Timothy Johnes and his contemporaries in Morristown testifying to the accuracy of the story. There was some uncertainty among these writers as to the year of the episode (1777 or 1780)[38] and as to the exact place where it had occurred (in an orchard near the parsonage, in a grove immediately behind Dr. Johnes' house, or under an apple tree).[39] It was generally agreed, however, that since the church was being used as an army hospital at the time, the service Washington attended was held outdoors (while "the cold winter winds whistled over the heads of the people").[40] Eventually, a large painting by Harry A. Ogden depicting Washington receiving communion under the apple tree was placed in the Presbyterian hospital in Philadelphia and a sundial marking the spot was placed by the Daughters of the American Revolution in the orchard behind the parsonage.[41]

Like the Valley Forge tale, the Morristown story has been told and retold with a steadily increasing proliferation of detail through the years. Washington, it turns out, attended services in the Morristown church more than once. He was, we learn, a "constant attendant" on Timothy Johnes' preaching;[42] he also asked Timothy's advice on numerous occasions and the two were "on the most friendly terms."[43] Washington was, not unexpectedly, always a "perfect gentleman" and he impressed the congregation with his "unvarying courteousness."[44] One Sunday, it was said, *Washington was there sitting in his camp chair brought in for the occasion. During the service, a woman came into the congregation with a child in her arms; Washington arose from his chair and gave it to the woman with the child."*[45]

Washington certainly could have attended a service at the Morristown church during the Revolution. Theologically, he had, as the story put it, no "exclusive partialities"; and from time to time he did attend churches other than the Anglican church of which he was a member. The request for the sacrament, however, is extremely dubious, for there are strong reasons for doubting that Washington was in the habit of participating in the sacrament, even in his own church. And like the Potts story, the Morristown episode, even in its simplest form, rests on nothing more than oral tradition. There is no reference to Timothy Johnes in any of Washington's extensive writings. And the indefatigable efforts of nineteenth-century authors to locate a written record of some kind substantiating the tale invariably ended in frustration and failure. Like the Valley Forge prayer and all the other legends about Washington in a pietistic posture, it has stubbornly resisted all efforts to track down evidence establishing its authenticity.

In 1831, for the first time, the treatment of Washington's religion by Weems and other evangelical-minded chroniclers came in for sharp criticism; and thereafter the pietists were to find themselves increasingly on the defensive. Bird Wilson, Episcopal minister in Albany, New York, was one of the first openly to challenge in public the pietistic picture of Washington that was being built up by Weems and his followers. In a sermon delivered in October, 1831, which attracted wide attention when it was reported in the *Albany Daily Advertiser,* Wilson stated flatly that "among all our presidents from Washington downward, not one was a professor of religion, at least not of more than unitarianism." Washington, he went on to say, was "a great and good man, but he was not a professor of religion"; he was really a typical eighteenth-century Deist, not a Christian, in his religious outlook. Wilson also declared that Dr. James Abercrombie, assistant rector of Christ Church in Philadelphia, which Washington attended while President, had confided to him that Washington never partook of the sacrament of the Lord's Supper during his presidency. On sacrament days, Wilson quoted Abercrombie as saying, "Washington's custom was to rise, just before the ceremony commenced, and to walk out of church."[46] About the time that Wilson was making his revelations from the pulpit, Frances Wright was announcing boldly from the lecture platform that "Washington was not a Christian—that is, he believed not in the priest's God, nor in the divine authority of the priest's book";[47] and Robert Dale Owen, in a long debate with Rev. Origen Bacheler, carried on in the columns of the *New York Free Enquirer,* was going to considerable lengths to disprove the popular picture of Washington as a devout Christian.[48]

The lines drawn in the Bacheler-Owen debate were clearcut. For Bacheler, Washington was

a man who recognized the Scriptures as *revelation,* and their author as *divine;* who was a member of a Christian church, and constant in his attendance on public worship; who was habituated to the reading of the Scriptures as a religious duty, and to acts of private devotion; and who, to his dying moment, remained stedfast in his religious views.[49]

But for Owen, "Washington's religion was of the most liberal stamp . . . the father of his country . . . died as he had lived, in dignity and peace; but he left behind him not one word to warrant the belief that he was other than a sincere deist."[50] In his quest for ammunition to use against Bacheler, Owen, having read reports of Bird Wilson's remarks about Washington, called on the Albany minister and read him extracts from the news story about his sermon. "When I had completed," reported Owen, "he said: 'I endorse every word of that.' He further added: 'As I conceive that truth is truth, whether it makes for or against us, I will not conceal from you any information on the subject, even such as I have not yet given to the public." Wilson then informed Owen that Dr. Abercrombie, whom he believed to have been in a position to speak with some authority, had once told him: "*Sir, Washington was a deist!*" Continuing, Wilson declared emphatically:

I have diligently perused every line that Washington ever gave to the public, and I do not find one expression in which he pledges himself as a professor of Christianity. I think any man who will candidly do as I have done, will come to the conclusion that he was a deist, and nothing more. I do not take upon myself to say positively that he was, but that is my opinion.[51]

If Owen's jubilant report of his interview with Wilson dismayed Bacheler, the latter showed no signs of it in his rejoinder. He continued to bolster the case for Washington's orthodoxy by citing the various legends that had grown up around Washington since Weems's day. But he had also done some researches of his own; and in replying to Owen he was apparently able to score a point by referring to a communication which he had received from Dr. Abercrombie himself. He was not at liberty to make the letter public, Bacheler explained, because the former rector of Christ Church did not wish "to appear before the public in print." Nevertheless, he could say this much: in his letter, Abercrombie "denied any recollection" of having told Wilson that Washington was a Deist and he also assured Bacheler that Washington was "a practicing Christian, though he did not commune in his church."[52] Bacheler was not, of course, satisfied with the latter part of Abercrombie's statement; and he proceeded to quote from another letter he had received on the subject of the sacrament. Rev. William Jackson of Alexandria, Virginia, he declared, had written him to say that "Universal tradition in the families of those whose parents or friends were acquainted with the general, is, that he was a regular communicant."[53] This closed the case, so far as Bacheler was concerned, and it remained only to dispose of Bird Wilson: "I have but to add . . . that it appears . . . that Rev. Dr. Wilson is an opposer of revivals of religion. This circumstance will have its proper weight with the public, whenever they think of his concessions to Mr. Owen."[54]

Bacheler's summary of the gist of Abercrombie's letter to him, we now know, was something less than candid. Abercrombie's exact words (which came to light many years later) were these:

Of the assertions made by Dr. Wilson in the conclusion of a paragraph of your letter, I cannot say I have the least recollection of such a conversation, but had I made use of the expression stated, it could not have extended farther than the expression of a private individual opinion. That Washington was a professing Christian is evident from his regular attendance in our church; but, Sir, I cannot consider any man as a real Christian who uniformly disregards an ordinance so solemnly enjoined by the divine Author of our holy religion, and considered as a challenge of divine grace. This, Sir, is all I think it proper to state on paper. In a conversation, more latitude being allowed, more light might, perhaps, be thrown upon it. I trust, however, Sir, you will not introduce my name in print.[55]

Bacheler, understandably, refrained from seeking further light on the subject from Abercrombie; and the controversy with Owen, who did not pursue the matter further, came to an end.

Nevertheless, the questions raised during the Bacheler-Owen controversy about Washington's orthodoxy led the pietists to redouble their efforts to demonstrate that Parson Weems's portrayal of Washington was an accurate one. The testimony of Bird Wilson they largely ignored; and from local legends and traditions, from painstaking exegesis of Washington texts, and from the statements of countless elderly persons who had vague memories of having seen Washington in a religious stance in the old days, the pietists gradually built up a case for Washington's evangelical fervor that went far beyond Weems's lively little fables about Washington's piety.

The first notable fruit of the new pietistic endeavor was Rev. Edward G. McGuire's *The Religious Opinions and Character of Washington*, the longest, most ambitious, and most influential of all the books ever published on the subject of Washington's religious behavior. Appearing in 1836, the book was directed specifically against "distinguished persons in our land" who had recently "evinced a strange anxiety"[56] to cast doubts on Washington's "evangelical convictions"[57] and "the soundness of his theological tenets."[58] Everything is here: all the legends regarding Washington's piety that had been piling up ever since Weems first ventured, somewhat cautiously (it would now seem), into the field, plus a variety of new anecdotes about Washington's praying habits which McGuire had collected on his own. So extravagant, indeed, were McGuire's claims and so padded was the book with irrelevant quotations and homiletic asides, that even the *New York Review and Quarterly Church Journal,* in basic sympathy with McGuire's purposes, felt obliged to chide the author for having "done great injury to his subject" by his excesses[59] and for having "exposed himself to some laughter."[60] But McGuire had done his work well; and his book became a prime source for subsequent pietistic publications on Washington.[61]

McGuire was especially skilful at extracting rich details about Washington's religious life from what, at first glance, might seem to be fairly unrewarding source material. His method became standard with later writers. Washington's library, for example, contained books on religion—Sir Matthew Hale's *Contemplations, Moral and Divine* was McGuire's chief exhibit—and this fact by itself became prima facie evidence of the first President's religiosity. (That he also possessed books by Voltaire and Paine was not regarded as relevant to the inquiry.) By quoting extensively from the book in question—McGuire reproduced about twenty pages of extracts from Hale's *Contemplations,* which he called Washington's *"vade mecum"*—it was possible to convey the impression that the views set forth in the quoted passages represented the considered opinions of Washington himself.[62] Washington's will, to take another example, began with the customary invocation of the period: "In the name of God, Amen." This phrase was seized upon by evangelical writers following McGuire's lead as indisputable proof of Washington's theism.[63] Or, to take a final example, if Washington happened to mention Christmas in his diary, this could be taken as incontrovertible evidence that he was "a true Christian in every sense that the word implies...."[64]

Perhaps the most ingenious—better still, astonishing—use of McGuire's extrapolative technique was made by Joseph Buffington, a century later, in a speech he made in 1932 which he later expanded into a book entitled *The Soul of Washington*.[65] Buffington began where McGuire had left off. Pointing out that Sir Matthew Hale, Chief Justice of King's Bench,* was a faithful churchgoer, he mused: "Was Washington inspired to his regular attendance at church when home and to Divine Service in Camp by the example of the Chief Justice, who, the story tells, never, in thirty-six years, missed a Sunday at church?"[66] But the plot thickens. Hale, according to Buffington, was known to have had a "remarkable devotion" to Christmas.[67] Was it not possible that Washington's "veneration for Christmas" was also fostered by the Chief Justice?[68] At the age of thirteen, Buff-

---

*In 1671 Sir Matthew Hale (1609-1676) was made Chief Justice of King's Bench, where he presided with distinction for several years. *Contemplations, Moral and Divine*, a collection of hortatory discourses together with a series of heroic couplets on Christmas, was first published shortly after his death and reprinted in 1700. Washington Irving, perhaps influenced by McGuire, declared that the "admirable maxims" in Hale's *Contemplations* "sank deep into the mind of George, and doubtless, had a great influence in forming his character." (Washington Irving, *Life of George Washington* [8 vols.; New York, 1857], I, 30.)

ington reminded his readers, Washington made a copy of some verses on Christmas which began:

> Assist me, Muse divine, to sing the Morn,
>   On which the Saviour of Mankind was born.[69]

That this was a clear indication of Washington's orthodoxy goes without saying; but Buffington had an even more interesting point to make. "Hale's veneration for Christmas [and] Washington's Christmas poem," he continued, "seem to me to have found fruitage in the Christmas Day Battle of Trenton, which was the turning point of the Revolution."[70]

> The dash was conceived by Washington, was made possible in his mind, and was successfully carried out by him because, filled with the Christmas spirit himself ... [and] knowing the German and British love of Christmas and their joy of Christmas cheer, Washington wisely reasoned that the Hessians, with memories of Christmas carols and feast and family gatherings in their homeland, would, of all nights in the year, be off guard. . . . never dreaming as they looked over the white plains of New Jersey, or saw the angry Delaware running wild with huge cakes of ice, that there could be such a thing as a dash from Pennsylvania.[71]

What would have happened had John Hancock, who came from a Puritan colony which did not celebrate Christmas, been chosen Commander in Chief, instead of Washington, Buffington hardly dared to speculate. For without the Christmas spirit, learned in a pious household when he was a boy and strengthened by the example of Sir Matthew Hale, Washington could scarcely have directed the Revolutionary struggle to its ultimate triumph.[72] Surely Weems and McGuire themselves never made a more remarkable union of piety and patriotism in treating of Washington.

At one point in *The Soul of Washington* Buffington catches himself up short: there is a danger, it suddenly occurs to him, that his readers will infer from all the instances of Washington's religious zeal he is presenting that Washington was "almost a religious fanatic."[73] He then hastens to assure the reader that Washington's was no "blind, supine" faith and that it was always kept within the bounds of decorous respectability.[74] Like McGuire, of course, Buffington wanted simply to demonstrate the "substantial agreement" of Washington's religious beliefs with "those of the great body of orthodox believers, in every age and country."[75] But like McGuire and the other pietists, Buffington, carried away by enthusiasm for his subject, ended by proving too much and, as the *New York Review* said of McGuire, exposing himself "to some laughter." The simple, sentimental Washington of Weems, whose "GREAT TALENTS" were "CONSTANTLY GUIDED AND GUARDED BY RELIGION,"[76] was gradually transformed by religious devotees into a figure so obsessed by devout observances that he might well, as Buffington feared, be considered "almost a religious fanatic." That Washington himself was, in fact, almost the exact opposite of a religious zealot can only be considered a tribute to the ingenuity of the pietistic folklorists.

What, then, are we to say about Washington's actual religious faith and practices? It is clear that the popular legends about Washington—the Valley Forge and the Morristown stories and the innumerable tales of Washington at prayer—must be dismissed as totally lacking in any kind of evidence that would hold up in a court of law. All of them, as Rev. Frank L. Humphreys somewhat reluctantly acknowledged in a sermon delivered in 1932, are of "doubtful hearsay quality."[77] But what positively can we say about Washington's religion? How much of a churchman was he? What was his conception of the role of organized religion in society? And what were his religious views as revealed in his private letters and in public statements? Can we, finally, after examining all the evidence, regard him as a Christian? Or was Bird Wilson correct in assuming that Washington was essentially a Deist?

II

WASHINGTON AS A CHURCHMAN

AFTER Washington's death, various religious groups with which he had been associated only in a casual way during his lifetime began competing with one another in claiming the first President as their own. Among Catholics, the tradition developed that Washington became a Roman Catholic shortly before he died or at least "was thinking of such a step before death overcame him."[1] Baptists, on the other hand, insisted that Washington regarded Baptist chaplains as "the most prominent and useful" in the Revolutionary army[2] and that in due course he requested baptism at the hands of Chaplain John Gano and was immersed in the Potomac River in the presence of forty-two witnesses.[3] The Swedenborgians, for their part, while not insisting upon Washington's formal membership in the Church of the New Jerusalem, declared that he was especially sympathetic to their point of view and that he was an avid reader of Emanuel Swedenborg's theological tomes.[4] Similarly, the

Universalists, while acknowledging that Washington was "not a professed Universalist," found in his public utterances overpowering evidence that he was essentially of their persuasion.[5]

Other denominations were more modest in their claims. Lutheran chroniclers asserted that Washington frequently attended the Zion Lutheran Church in Philadelphia and was "much impressed by the dignity of the service"[6] and that, further, he was a close friend of Rev. John Peter Gabriel Muhlenberg, "with whom he often shot bucks in the Blue Ridge Mountains";[7] German Reformed writers that he regularly attended the Reformed church when he was in Germantown, Pennsylvania, and that he once took communion with the congregation;[8] Methodist writers that he voiced high regard for John Wesley[9] and that he had "many personal and friendly interviews" with Bishop Francis Asbury;[10] and Jewish writers that he was present at a Jewish marriage ceremony on one occasion,[11] ate a kosher meal on another,[12] and on a third delivered a speech which had been originally composed in rabbinical Hebrew.[13] The Presbyterians, of course, had the Morristown story, though, as has been pointed out, its popularity was not confined to Presbyterian circles.

Of the major religious bodies in the United States, only two refrained from embroidering the record of their associations with the first President: the Quakers, who could scarcely claim Washington as a pacifist Friend, and the Episcopalians, who were quite satisfied with the actual facts of Washington's denominational attachments.

The facts were plain enough and it is possible to speak of Washington's activities and behavior as a churchman with a considerable degree of exactitude. He was baptized and married in the Anglican church in Virginia and, while he did attend and make contributions to other churches from time to time during his public life, he was a lifelong member and supporter of the church into which he had been born. Like his father before him, he served actively for many years as one of the twelve vestrymen for Truro parish, Virginia, in which Mount Vernon was located.

According to Charles H. Callahan, "The regularity of his attendance at the meetings of the vestry and the progress of church work throughout the parish during his incumbency is a striking testimonial of the religious zeal and activity of him and his associates."[14] Actually, under the Anglican establishment in Virginia before the Revolution, the duties of a parish vestry were as much civil as religious in nature and it is not possible to deduce any exceptional religious zeal from the mere fact of membership. Even Thomas Jefferson was a vestryman for a while.* Consisting of the leading gentlemen of the parish in position and influence (many of whom, like Washington, were also at one time or other members of the County Court and of the House of Burgesses), the parish vestry, among other things, levied the parish taxes, handled poor relief, fixed land boundaries in the parish, supervised the construction, furnishing, and repairs of churches, and hired ministers and paid their salaries. Each year the vestry selected two of its members

---

*As Bishop William Meade put it, somewhat nastily, in 1857: "Even Mr. Jefferson, and [George] Wythe, who did not conceal their disbelief in Christianity, took their parts in the duties of vestrymen, the one at Williamsburg, the other at Albemarle; for they wished to be men of influence." (William Meade, *Old Churches, Ministers and Families of Virginia* [2 vols.; Philadelphia, 1857], I, 191).

to serve as churchwardens, with special duties to perform, such as binding out orphans and indigent children as apprentices and presenting cases of blasphemy, profanity, drunkenness, adultery, and fornication to the County Court.[15]

Washington was an active member of Truro vestry from 1763 until 1774 and a nominal member until 1784, when he submitted his resignation.[16] On three occasions during his active years he also served as one of the churchwardens. When, in February, 1765, Truro parish was divided and Mount Vernon was included in the new parish of Fairfax, Washington was elected a vestryman for Fairfax. With the restoration of Mount Vernon to Truro parish a few months later, he resigned from the Fairfax vestry and was elected again to the vestry of Truro. He did not, as Jared Sparks and many writers after him have asserted—as an instance of his "lively interest in Church affairs"—serve in two parishes at the same time.[17]

Being a vestryman was an accepted duty for a gentleman of his social status and Washington seems to have performed his parish duties faithfully: serving on church building committees, handling the parish collection, and selling parish tobacco. But it is impossible to read any special religious significance into his service.[18] If he accepted without reservations—and indeed profited socially by—the union of church and state inherent in the Anglican parish system before the Revolution, he also accepted without protest the dissolution of the system that came with the disestablishment of the Virginia church following the Revolutionary War. There were staunch churchmen like Edmund Pendleton who fought hard against disestablishment, but Washington was not among them.[19]

Before the Revolution Washington owned two pews in Pohick Church, about seven miles from Mount Vernon, and one pew in Christ Church in Alexandria. It was Pohick Church that he was in the habit of attending before the war; in 1785 he shifted to the Alexandria church.[20] Rev. Lee Massey was rector of Pohick Church before the Revolution, and Parson Weems quoted him as saying:

I never knew so constant an attendant at Church as Washington. His behavior in the House of God was ever so deeply reverential, and greatly assisted me in my pulpit labors. No company ever withheld him from church. I have often been at Mount Vernon, on Sabbath morning, when his breakfast table was filled with guests; but to him they furnished no pretext for neglecting his God, and losing the satisfaction of setting a good example. For instead of staying home out of false complaisance to them, he used constantly to invite them to accompany him.[21]

But Massey's statement was made many years after the period to which he referred and, as Paul Leicester Ford suggested, it was probably made "more with an eye to its influence on others than to its strict accuracy."[22] The same comment may be made of George Washington Parke Custis' statement, some years after Washington's death, that his step-grandfather "was always a strict and decorous observer of the Sabbath. He invariably attended divine service once a day, when within reach of a place of worship."[23]

If we examine Washington's own record of what he did on Sunday before the Revolution, we find that he was considerably less conscientious about attending church than either Lee Massey or G.W.P. Custis seems to have recollected. According to his diary, Washington went to church four times during the first five months of 1760 and in 1768 he went fifteen times; and these years seem to be fairly typical of the period from 1760 to 1773.[24] It is true, as the pietists have noted, that bad weather sometimes made it impossible to make the trip to church, that illness occasionally kept Washington at home, and that Pohick Church did not hold services every Sunday because the rector had to preach elsewhere in Truro parish. But Washington, we know, also transacted business on Sundays, visited friends and relatives, traveled, and sometimes went fox-hunting instead of going to church.[25] Frequently, also, during the 1760's, he wrote that on Sunday he stayed "at Home alone all day."[26] Moreover, of his churchgoing, Washington, in one of his rare playful moods, wrote to a friend in 1762:

I was favoured with your Epistle wrote on a certain 25th of July when you ought to have been at Church, praying as becomes every good Christian Man who has as much to answer for as you have; strange it is that you will be so blind to truth, that the enlightning sounds of the Gospel cannot reach your Ear, nor no Examples awaken you to a sense of Goodness; could you but behold with what religious zeal I hye me to Church on every Lords day, it would do your heart good, and fill it with equal fervency. . . .[27]

It is one of the few comments that Washington ever made on his church attendance.

Washington may have attended church more faithfully after his marriage in 1759 to Martha Custis, herself a devout churchwoman, as John C. Fitzpatrick believed. But at the most it does not seem to have exceeded an average of once a month. During the Stamp Act crisis, however, and on the eve of the break with Britain he attended church more regularly than usual. During 1774, for example, he went to

church twice and sometimes three times a month. And
during the Revolution he saw to it that divine services
were performed by the chaplains as regularly as possible
on the Sabbath for the soldiers under his command.[28]

As President, Washington attended St. Paul's Chapel
(or sometimes Trinity Church) in New York City and
Christ Church (or, from time to time, St. Peter's) in Philadelphia just about every Sunday. But once back at Mount
Vernon after his retirement he lapsed into his pre-Revolutionary habit of attending church about once a month. In
1799, the year of his death, he wrote:

> Six days do I labour, or, in other words, take exercise and
> devote my time to various occupations in Husbandry, and about
> my mansion. On the seventh, now called the first day, for want
> of a place of Worship (within less than nine miles) such letters
> as do not require immediate acknowledgment I give answers
> to.... But it hath so happened, that on the two last Sundays,
> call them the first or the seventh day as you please, I have been
> unable to perform the latter duty, on account of visits from
> Strangers, with whom I could not use the freedom to leave alone,
> or recommend to the care of each other, for their amusement.[29]

John C. Fitzpatrick's summation of Washington's churchgoing habits (which he examined carefully) seems fair
enough: "Washington ... was a consistent, if not always
regular churchgoer."[30]

Of Washington's reaction to the sermons he heard in
the various churches he attended during his life there is
very little that we can say. He was not in the habit of
recording in his diary either the name of the preacher or
the subject of the sermon which he heard. On only three
occasions did he go into any detail about the services he

attended. One Sunday in November, 1789, while traveling in Connecticut, he mentioned attending church twice ("It being contrary to law and disagreeable to the people of this State to travel on the Sabbath day") and hearing "very lame discourses from a Mr. Pond."[31] There is also an entry in his diary for July 3, 1791, when he was in York, Pennsylvania, in which he stated that

there being no Episcopal minister present in this place, I went to hear morning Service performed in the Dutch reformed Church —which, being in that language not a word of which I understood I was in no danger of becoming a proselyte to its religion by the eloquence of the Preacher.[32]

And in October, 1794, at the time of the Whiskey Rebellion, he wrote that he attended a Presbyterian church in Carlisle, Pennsylvania, and heard a "political Sermon" on "order and good government" preached by Dr. Robert Davidson.[33] But the usual entry in his diary is quite perfunctory: "Went to Pohick Church and returned to dinner;" "Went up to Alexandria Church;" "St. Paul's, N. Y."[34]

Two days before Washington retired from the presidency, the rector, churchwardens, and vestrymen of the United Episcopal Churches of Christ and St. Peter's in Philadelphia presented him with a congratulatory address in which they stated that "we feel a peculiar source of sensibility in the circumstance of your having attended divine worship among us; as well during your Presidency, as on many preceding occasions of your temporary residence in this city." "I have been gratified, during my residence among you," Washington told them politely, "by the liberal and interesting discourses which have been delivered in your Churches."[35] But, as Bishop White pointed out some years afterward, there was nothing in Washington's statement that "committed him relatively to religious theory."[36]

On May 24, 1774, the Virginia Assembly, whose sessions Washington was attending in Williamsburg, voted to observe a day of fasting, humiliation, and prayer on the first day of June to demonstrate its sympathy with Massachusetts on the day that the Boston Port Bill went into effect. Washington, accordingly, noted in his diary on June 1: "Went to Church and fasted all day."[37] Here, as elsewhere, there have been attempts to read profound spiritual significance into Washington's notation. "Will the reader mark especially the latter clause of this note," exclaimed one writer.

He went to church in conformity with the order passed by the house of burgesses. But not only so—he did that also which, perhaps, was not known to any mortal; which was known only to God,—*he fasted all day*. Who is not struck with the sincerity and piety of this account?[38]

And another writer referred to the seven words in Washington's diary as "seven lights, the seven golden candles so to speak, that throw a most penetrating light into the deeper and spiritual life of this great man."[39] But Washington's action on that day, like that of other Virginians, was of course politically, not religiously, motivated.

As to Washington's behavior in church, Eleanor Parke ("Nelly") Custis, Martha Washington's granddaughter, who resided at Mount Vernon for many years and attended church with the Washingtons, declared: "No one in church attended to the services with more reverential respect."[40] William White, who officiated at Christ Church in Philadelphia during and after the Revolution and who was one of the chaplains in Congress during Washington's presidency, made a similar comment. Washington, he assured an inquirer in 1832, was "always serious and attentive" in church. But he added that he never saw Washington kneeling during the services.[41] Nelly Custis also declared that Washington "always stood during the devotional parts of the service."[42]

Regarding the Lord's Supper, we have the firsthand testimony of three witnesses in a position to know what they were talking about—Nelly Custis, Bishop White, and Dr. James Abercrombie, assistant rector of Christ Church in Philadelphia—that Washington was not in the habit of partaking of the sacrament. "On communion Sundays," according to Mrs. Custis, "he left the church with me, after the blessing, and returned home, and we sent the carriage back for my grandmother."[43] In 1835, Bishop White, in answer to Colonel Hugh Mercer's question as to "whether General Washington was a *regular communicant* in the Episcopal Church in Philadelphia," replied: "In regard to the subject of your inquiry, truth requires me to say, that General Washington never received the communion, in the churches of which I am parochial minister. Mrs. Washington was an habitual communicant."[44] And Dr. Abercrombie had an even more interesting story to tell about Washington and the sacrament. It appeared in his letter to Origen Bacheler in 1831 and Bacheler, for obvious reasons, chose not to make it public:

...observing that on Sacrament Sundays, Gen'l Washington immediately after the Desk and Pulpit services, went out with the greater part of the congregation, always leaving Mrs. Washington with the communicants, she *invariably* being one, I considered it my duty, in a sermon on Public Worship, to state the unhappy tendency of *example*, particularly those in elevated stations, who invariably turned their backs upon the celebration of the Lord's Supper. I acknowledge the remark was intended for the President, as such, he received it. A few days later, in conversation with, I believe, a Senator of the U.S., he told me he had dined the day before with the President, who in the course of the conversation at the table, said, that on the preceding Sunday, he had received a very just reproof from the pulpit, for always leaving the church before the administration of the Sacrament; that he honored the preacher for his integrity and candour; that he had never considered the influence of his example; that he would never again give cause for the repetition of the reproof; and that, as he had never been a communicant, were he to become one of them, it would be imputed to an ostentatious display of religious zeal arising altogether from his elevated station. Accordingly, he afterwards never came on the morning of Sacrament Sunday, tho' at other times, a constant attendant in the morning.[45]

Abercrombie's report that Washington "had never been a communicant," together with the statements of Mrs. Custis and Bishop White, surely must be regarded as conclusive. It is reluctant testimony and as such carries a high degree of credibility. Neither White nor Abercrombie had anything to gain by their revelations; Abercrombie, indeed, was admittedly displeased by Washington's behavior. But like Bird Wilson, they seem to have believed (as Wilson told Robert Dale Owen) that "truth is truth, whether it makes for or against us" and one can only respect them—and Washington—for their candor.[46] By contrast, the various stories collected by the pietists to prove that Washington received the sacrament at Morristown and elsewhere are based on mere hearsay statements made many years after Washington's death.[47]

Most of the pietists have simply ignored the White-Abercrombie testimony. But it is interesting to note that William Dunlap, Canon of Washington Cathedral, one of the few to take it into consideration, once suggested that

Washington entertained such a vivid appreciation of the grace received through participating in the sacrament of the Lord's Supper as to warrant his refraining from participating in it when circumstances or temperament led him to believe he was not through preparation of mind and heart in the proper condition for its reception.[48]

It is quite probable that at no time in his life—though we have no firsthand evidence of any kind for the pre-Revolutionary period—did Washington consider his mind and heart in a proper condition to receive the sacrament. Hypocrisy is surely no Christian virtue; and the pietists might well have applauded Washington's basic honesty and integrity in this matter.

If Washington did not partake of the sacrament, he did, on occasion, observe the custom of having a blessing pronounced at mealtime. If he was giving a public dinner and there was a clergyman present, Washington invariably asked him to say grace. Claude Blanchard, Commissary of the French Auxiliary Army in the United States, dined with Washington and his staff at Peekskill, New York, on July 1, 1781, and he observed that there "was a clergyman at this dinner who blessed the food and said grace after they had done eating and brought on the wine." "I was told," Blanchard added, "that General Washington said grace when there was no clergyman at the table, as fathers of a family do in America." But Blanchard was not entirely convinced. "The first time I dined with him," he wrote,

there was no clergyman and I did not perceive that he made this prayer; yet I remember that, on taking his place at table, he made a gesture and said a word which I took for a piece of politeness, and which perhaps was a religious action. In this case, his prayer must have been short; the clergyman made use of more forms.[49]

It may have been such a "brief gesture" that Senator Paine Wingate of New Hampshire observed when he attended a dinner held in Martha Washington's honor in New York City shortly after Washington's inauguration in 1789. "As there was no chaplain present," he wrote afterward, "the President himself said a very short grace as he was sitting down."[50] On the other hand, Ashbel Green, Presbyterian minister in Philadelphia and, with Bishop White, one of the chaplains in Congress while Washington was President, was emphatic in his insistence that Washington always said grace himself when no clergyman was present. In his memoirs, published in 1849, Green recalled that it was "the usage under President Washington's administration that the chaplains of congress should dine with him once every month, while congress was in session." At one such dinner, according to Green,

the President's mind was probably occupied with some interesting concern, and on going to the table he began to ask a blessing himself. He uttered but a word or two, when bowing to me, he requested me to proceed, which I accordingly did. I mention this because it shows that President Washington always asked a blessing himself, when a chaplain wasn't present.[51]

The "word or two" uttered by Washington on this occasion may well have been in the nature of a blessing, as Green interpreted them; but it is doubtless going too far—as it always is with Washington—to infer from the episode that Washington "always asked a blessing himself, when a chaplain wasn't present."

A story similar to Green's was related by Rev. Alexander McWhir, Presbyterian minister and educator, some years after Washington's death. After the Revolution McWhir was in charge of a school in Alexandria of which Washington was a trustee, and he had occasion to visit Mount Vernon from time to time to discuss the affairs of the school.[52] Once, according to McWhir, Washington

called upon me to ask a blessing before meat. When the cloth was about to be removed, he returned thanks himself. Mrs. Washington, with a smile, said,—"My dear, you forgot that you had a clergyman dining with you today." With equal pleasantness, he replied, "My dear, I wish clergymen and all men to know that I am not a *graceless* man."[53]

It is certainly possible that some such incident took place at Mount Vernon. But it is also quite clear that the remark attributed to Washington was entirely out of character. Washington was simply not in the habit of making public pronouncements about his religious habits. If he stubbornly refused to participate in the sacrament of the Lord's Supper in the face of criticism from the pulpit, he was not likely to be concerned that "clergymen and all men" know that he always said grace at mealtime.

We have, moreover, evidence that even on public occasions, when no clergyman was present, Washington omitted the blessing. Congressman Roger Griswold of Connecticut attended a dinner given by the Washingtons for the delegations from Connecticut and Maryland, and in a letter from Philadelphia to his wife, dated January 1, 1796, he reported: "Six servants in livery attended at the table. We had no grace."[54] And Amariah Frost, one of the Justices of the Court of General Sessions at Worcester, Massachusetts, who dined at Mount Vernon on June 26, 1797, wrote in his diary afterward: "The President directed us where to sit (no grace was said)."[55]

A favorite source for those seeking evidence that Washington always said grace at meals in his own household has been a book published by an Englishman, Major James Walter. Major Walter arrived in the United States in 1882 with three portraits—two of Washington and one of Martha —which he announced were originals done by James Sharples, an English artist who is known to have painted Washington sometime after his retirement from office in March, 1797. The portraits were placed on exhibition on two different occasions in the Boston Art Museum, and Major Walter hoped to interest the United States government in purchasing them.[56] In 1887 he published a book entitled *Memorials of Washington and Mary, His Mother, and Martha, His Wife,* purportedly based upon the letters and papers of Sharples himself and on those of Robert Cary, Washington's business agent in London before the Revolution. It was Cary, according to Major Walter, who commissioned Sharples to execute the Washington portraits which he was exhibiting in Boston.[57] Walter's primary object in publishing *Memorials* was to present evidence from the correspondence of Washington, Cary, and Sharples himself, that the portraits in his possession were Sharples originals.

But in the course of the book there appeared an extract from one of Sharples' letters that has been quoted extensively in support of the contention that Washington observed the custom of saying grace in the privacy of his home:

> I take all my meals with the Chief at Mount Vernon; they are most elegantly served, but without the least profusion, and the attendance is of military precision. I observed that we never partook of food without the General offering grace to the Giver, so also at the close of every repast.[58]

Unfortunately for Major Walter, however, everything in his book, including this passage, was eventually rejected as spurious by the Massachusetts Historical Society. A committee of investigation, headed by Francis Parkman, in a delightfully written report published in 1888, demonstrated beyond a shadow of doubt not only that the portraits were fakes but also that the documents appearing in *Memorials* (for which Walter could produce no originals) all bore "the unmistakable stamp of the Walterian style."[59] With the elimination of Sharples, we are left with no contemporary witness to the fact that Washington ever pronounced a blessing at meals in his own household.

On this much discussed question, then, we can only conclude: Washington always asked a clergyman to say grace at meals; and, sometimes, on public occasions, when there was no clergyman at the table, he may have done so himself. More than this, we cannot say.

What about Washington's attitude toward the Bible? Washington, it has been said, cultivated a "sacred intimacy" with the Bible.[60] "Line upon line," according to Eliphalet Potter, "precept upon precept, by faithful practice he made his own the letter and spirit of that sublime Book which he read devotedly and prized supremely."[61] If this is so, there are astonishingly few references to the Bible in his letters and public statements.

At the end of the Revolutionary War, when John Rodgers, Presbyterian minister in New York City and for a time chaplain in the army, wrote to suggest a distribution of Bibles among the soldiers of the Continental Army, Washington expressed his approval of giving "such an important present, to the brave fellows." But he explained that a majority of the men had already been discharged and that "it is now too late to make the Attempt."[62] In 1792, when the "Self-Interpreting Bible" of John Brown of Haddington, a Scotch Presbyterian, was published in New York, the list of subscribers was headed by "George Washington, Esq., President of the United States of America."[63] The John Brown Bible had a wide circulation in the United States, but we have no way of knowing what use Washington made of his own copy. One other Bible in Washington's possession deserves mention. In July, 1795, Washington wrote Rev. Clement Crutwell, an English author and compiler, acknowledging the receipt of the Bible of Rev. Thomas Wilson, Bishop of Sodor and Man (in three large folio volumes with notes), which had been willed to him by the Bishop's son;[64] and in his Last Will and Testament he directed that the Bible be given to his old friend Bryan Lord Fairfax. Much has been made by the pietists of Washington's possession of this Bible; but, really, all that we can say is that Washington received it and that he bequeathed it to Lord Fairfax.[65]

The only passage in Washington's writings which indicates that he had been reading portions of the Bible appears in a letter to Charles Thomson, former secretary of the Continental Congress, in March, 1795. Thomson had retired from public service after the Revolution to devote himself to translating the Septuagint and the New Testament, and he sent a copy of his translation of the former to Washington. Washington wrote to express his thanks and declared that he had read the "first part" of Thomson's translation.[66]

But Washington's allusions to the Scriptures elsewhere are few and far between. One expression—"vine and fig tree"—seems to have been a favorite with him. From time to time, during the Revolution and while he was President, he expressed to his friends an intense longing to be back at Mount Vernon "in the peaceable enjoyment of my own Vine and fig tree."[67] In notes which he jotted down in preparation for one of his public addresses, there also appears this passage:

The blessed Religion revealed in the word of God will remain an eternal and awful monument to prove that the best Institutions may be abused by human depravity; and that they may even, in some instances be made subservient to the vilest of purposes.[68]

But in the end, for whatever reason, he made no use of this, the only truly serious reference he ever made to the Bible. The only other references are humorous in tone.

In writing to Burwell Bassett in 1762, for example, he announced that his tobacco was "assailed by every villainous worm that has had an existence since the days of Noah (how unkind it was of Noah now I have mentioned his name to suffer such a brood of vermin to get a birth in the Ark)...."[69] And in a letter dated May, 1772, to

Jonathan Boucher, the Anglican clergyman who tutored Washington's stepson, John Parke ("Jacky") Custis, for a time (and who became a Loyalist during the Revolution), he declared: "Your excuse for denying us the pleasure of your Company . . . tho not strictly warranted by Scripture, is nevertheless highly admissable."[70] But his most extensive reference to biblical material is contained in a whimsical letter which he wrote to Mrs. Annis Boudinot Stockton on September 2, 1783, thanking her for a poem she had composed in his honor. Teasing her for the self-deprecating way in which she had referred to her poetical effort, Washington declared:

> You apply to me, My dear Madam, for absolution as tho' I was your father Confessor; and as tho' you had commited a crime, great in itself, yet of the venial class. You have reason good, for I find myself strangely disposed to be a very indulgent ghostly Adviser on this occasion; and, notwithstanding "you are the most offending Soul alive" (that is, if it is a crime to write elegant Poetry) yet if you will come and dine with me on Thursday and go through the proper course of penitence, which shall be prescribed, I will strive hard to assist you in expiating these poetical trespasses on this side of purgatory. Nay more, if it rests with me to direct your future lucubrations, I shall certainly urge you to a repetition of the same conduct, on purpose to shew you what an admirable knack you have at confession and reformation. . . .

Warming to his subject, Washington continued:

> You see Madam, when once Woman has tempted us and we have tasted the forbidden fruit, there is no such thing as checking our appetites, whatever the consequences may be. You will I dare say, recognize our being the genuine Descendants of those who are reputed to be our great Progenitors.

Having expressed his desire for more of her poetry in this bantering fashion, he went on, in the same vein, to deprecate himself as a subject for verse-making:

...to oblige you to make such an excellent Poem, on such a subject, without any Materials but those of simple reality, would be as cruel as the Edict of Pharaoh which compelled the Children of Israel to Manufacture Bricks without the necessary Ingredients. Thus are you sheltered under the authority of prescription, and I will not dare to charge you with an intentional breach of the Rules of the decalogue in giving so bright a colouring to the services I have been enabled to render my Country. . . .[71]

If Washington "diligently searched the Holy Volume," as has been asserted, he seems to have utilized his findings largely for purposes of whimsy.[72]

Taking Washington's religious practices as a whole, we can only conclude that the first President was considerably less orthodox than he has commonly been portrayed. By no stretch of the imagination would it seem possible to characterize his religious behavior as that of a dedicated evangelical. From the pietist point of view, it is clear, he was lukewarm, even cold, in the outward expression of his religious feelings. Even from the standpoint of a loyal (but nonevangelical) churchman like Bird Wilson, his abstention from the essential forms and conventions of his own church certainly left a good deal to be desired. It must not be inferred from this, however, that Washington was hostile to formal religious observances (even those in which he could not conscientiously bring himself to take part), or that he was in any serious respect an anticlerical. Quite the contrary. He always asked a clergyman to say grace, as we have seen; and he also expressed respect for Abercrombie's position on the sacrament. Moreover, he more than once, during his public career, stated his firm conviction that organized religion was an indispensable basis for both morality and social order. In both military and civil life, Washington was always insistent upon the importance of the role that religion had to perform in the lives of the people over whose destinies he was called upon to preside.

III

RELIGION AND THE SOCIAL ORDER

ONE DAY shortly after the close of the Revolution, it is said, Washington encountered a country parson "advancing towards him with bared head" and engaged him in conversation. "Put on your hat," said Washington, "and I will shake hands with you." "Not in the presence of one who has done so much for our country," replied the clergyman. "You did just as much," Washington insisted. "No, no," protested the clergyman. "We both did what we could," Washington concluded simply.[1]

Fanciful in itself, the anecdote does not err in picturing a cordial attitude on Washington's part toward ministers of the gospel. Throughout his public career, he regarded organized religion as an important stabilizing factor in society. He was, after all, reared in an environment that took the Anglican establishment for granted; and even after the separation of church and state had been effected in Virginia (and in the United States Constitution) he continued to

45

look hospitably upon institutionalized religion. In their eagerness to demolish the legends about Washington's devout observances, freethinkers have tended to ignore this aspect of Washington's thought. The plain fact is that Washington was neither an evangelical nor an anticlerical. In his attitude toward organized religion, if not in his own personal religious opinions, Washington was without question profoundly conservative. There was no "social gospel" in his outlook. The church, for Washington, was a conserving, not a reforming, force in society. He looked upon it as the bulwark of the American social and political order. It was the church's "laudable endeavours to render men sober, honest, and good citizens, and the obedient subjects of a lawful government" that Washington usually emphasized when speaking of religion in public.[2]

The most famous statement of Washington's views on the relation between religion and society is contained in his Farewell Address. "Of all the dispositions and habits which lead to political prosperity," Washington told his fellow-countrymen just before retiring from public life,

Religion and morality are indispensable supports.—In vain would that man claim the tribute of Patriotism, who should labour to subvert these great Pillars of human happiness, these firmest props of the duties of Men & citizens.—The mere Politician, equally with the pious man ought to respect & to cherish them. —A volume could not trace all their connections with private & public felicity.—Let it simply be asked where is the security for property, for reputation, for life, if the sense of religious obligation *desert* the oaths, which are the instruments of investigation in Courts of Justice?—And let us with caution indulge the supposition, that morality can be maintained without religion.— Whatever may be conceded to the influence of refined education

on minds of peculiar structure—reason & experience both forbid
us to expect that national morality can prevail in exclusion of
religious principle.[3]

Perhaps no passage in all of Washington's public statements has been quoted as frequently as this one to support
the contention that the first President was an orthodox
believer. "Hear this, ye reckless speculators in moon-
shine sentimentality," cried Origen Bacheler in one of his
exchanges with Robert Dale Owen,

—Hear a Washington pronouncing you to be void of patriotism
and dangerous members of society!... Washington uttered not
this sentiment merely as an *opinion*, but as a matter of *experience*.
He uttered it at the very period the *experiment* was *making* in
France. There, religion had been discarded, and national morality
went with it.[4]

In Washington's Farewell Address, declared Edward C.
McGuire,

we have a vindication of evangelical doctrines which cannot, we
think, be too highly estimated. A full development of the preg-
nant meaning of its statements, cannot fail to give entire assurance, not only of the faith of the writer in the truth of Christianity,
but also to impress us with the most gratifying views of the
accuracy and soundness of his theological tenets.[5]

Here, as always, McGuire was reading far too much into
Washington's words. Washington's reference was to religion
in general, not to Christianity in particular. Moreover, religion was upheld by him in this passage chiefly (if not solely)
for its social and national utility. It is worth remarking,
further, that even in an important public pronouncement

of this kind Washington refused to place the secular human-
ist entirely beyond the pale. The "influence of refined
education on minds of peculiar structure," he acknowledged,
might make possible a moral life unsupported by religious
sanctions. McGuire was somewhat troubled by the point,
but in the end he reassured himself. "This, however," he
declared, "is not positively asserted by the author, but as
it would seem, reluctantly 'conceded.' "[6] Washington did
indeed make his concession "with caution." Clearly, he
didn't think that morality ungrounded in religion would
work for most people. Still, it is difficult to see how McGuire
could conclude that the paragraph as a whole represented
"a view held only with decision, by the most evangelical
religious communions."[7] Presumably, to evangelicals like
McGuire, the significance of religion went far beyond the
social and patriotic purposes which were emphasized by
Washington.

The Farewell Address, as is well known, was based
largely upon material prepared for Washington by James
Madison and Alexander Hamilton (more especially the
latter), after Washington had made a rough draft of the
points which he wished to include in his valedictory. But
as Victor Paltsits pointed out in his analysis of the genesis
of the document:

> Throughout the preparation Washington's ideas or "senti-
> ments," as he liked to call them, were preserved. Hamilton knew,
> as Madison had before him, that whatever he might do in
> reshaping, rewriting, or forming anew a draft, the results should
> be "predicated upon the Sentiments" which Washington had
> indicated. ... In the last analysis, Washington was his own edi-
> tor; and what he published to the world as a Farewell Address,
> was in its final form in content what he had chosen to make it

by processes of adoption and adaptation. By this procedure every idea became his own without equivocation.[8]

What Paltsits says of the address as a whole unquestionably applies to the paragraph on religion. Though taken from what Paltsits called "Hamilton's original major draft" and utilized by Washington with only minor changes, it expressed perfectly a lifelong opinion of the first President's. Born into the Anglican church and, like most upper-class Virginians before the Revolution, looking upon the Anglican establishment as part of the natural order of things, Washington seems never during his life to have questioned the relevance of organized religion to social order and morality. Long before he became President of the United States, he had been keenly aware of the social uses of institutional religion. As a military leader during the French and Indian War and during the American Revolution, he looked upon religion as indispensable to the morale, discipline, and good conduct of the men under his command.

The pietists have understandably been charmed by the persistence with which Washington called for chaplains for the army in time of war. As commander of Virginia troops on the western frontier at the time of the French and Indian War, he was eager, from the start, to obtain the services of a chaplain for his regiment. A "Gentleman of sober, serious and religious deportment . . . chosen for this important Trust," he insisted, would improve discipline among his men, raise their morale, and check gambling, drinking, and swearing in the regiment.[9] "The want of a chaplain, does, I conceive, reflect dishonor upon the regiment . . . ," he wrote Robert Dinwiddie, Governor of Virginia, in one of several letters on the subject.[10] To John Blair, President of the Virginia Council, he declared with some exasperation: "Common decency, Sir, in a camp calls for the services of a divine, and which ought not to be dispensed with, altho' the world should be so uncharitable as to think us void of religion, and incapable of good instruction."[11] But Governor Dinwiddie was unable to find a clergyman willing to take the position, and the young colonel did the best he could by himself. He issued strict orders against "Swearing, getting Drunk, or using an Obscene Language"[12] and saw that his men marched to Sunday prayers as regularly as possible.[13]

Similarly, twenty years later, when he became Commander in Chief of the Continental Army, Washington was eager, from the very beginning, to provide the men under his command with a sufficient number of chaplains of "Character and good conversation."[14] When he arrived in Cambridge early in July, 1775, to take command of the troops around Boston, there were already a few chaplains attached to the different regiments sent from the various colonies. Some of them were volunteers, serving without pay; others had received regular appointments from the Massachusetts Provincial Congress.[15] One of them—Rev. Abiel Leonard of the Third Connecticut Regiment—seemed particularly to represent everything that Washington desired in a chaplain. "His General Conduct," he told Governor Jonathan Trumbull of Connecticut,

has been exemplary and praiseworthy: In discharging the duties of his Office, active and industrious; he has discovered himself a warm and steady friend to his Country, and taken great pains to animate the Soldiery and impress them with a knowledge of the important rights we are contending for. Upon the late desertion of the Troops, he gave a Sensible and judicious discourse, holding forth the Necessity of courage and bravery and at the same time of Obedience and Subordination to those in Command.[16]

Washington regarded the performance of these services as indispensable in the Continental Army.

On July 29, 1775, the Continental Congress, in its first official act regarding army chaplaincies, passed a resolution providing for a salary of twenty dollars a month for chaplains, the same as that for captains.[17] Washington regarded this as inadequate to attract competent clergymen. "I have long had it on my mind to mention to Congress," he wrote the President of Congress on December 31,

that frequent applications had been made to me respecting the Chaplain's pay, which is too small to encourage men of Abilities. Some of them who have left their Flocks, are Obliged to pay the parson acting for them more than they receive. I need not point out the great utility of Gentlemen whose lives and conversation are unexceptionable, being employed for that service in this Army. There are two ways of making it worth the Attention of such; one is, an advancement of their pay, the other, that one Chaplain should be appointed to two regiments; this last I think may be done without Inconvenience, I beg leave to recommend this matter to Congress whose sentiments thereon I shall impatiently expect.[18]

Congress adopted Washington's recommendations; and in his General Orders for February 7, 1776, he was able to announce that "there shall be one Chaplain to two Regiments, and that the pay of each Chaplain shall be *Thirty-three* dollars and *one third* pr Kalendar month."[19]

By June, however, the situation of the army had changed drastically, with the shifting of the theater of action from

New England to New York, and Washington wrote Congress again to suggest new arrangements:

The Army now being differently circumstanced from what it was, part here, part at Boston, and a third part detached to Canada, has Introduced much confusion and disorder in this Instance. nor do I know how it is possible to remedy the Evil, but by affixing one [chaplain] to each Regiment, with a salary competent to their support, no Shifting, no Change from one Regiment to another, can answer the purpose, and in many cases it could not be done, tho' the Regiments should consent, as where detachments are composed of unequal numbers, or Ordered from different Posts. Many more Inconveniences might be pointed out, but these it is presumed will sufficiently shew the defect of the present establishment and the propriety of an alteration. What that Alteration shall be Congress will please to determine.[20]

Again Congress acted on Washington's advice and authorized the appointment of one chaplain for each regiment at the prevailing salary. In his orders for July 9, 1776, therefore, Washington directed

the Colonels or commanding officers of each regiment ... to procure Chaplains accordingly; persons of good Characters and exemplary lives—To see that all inferior officers and soldiers pay them a suitable respect and attend carefully upon religious exercises. The blessing and protection of Heaven are at all times necessary but especially so in times of public distress and danger....[21]

The following year, Congress boosted the pay of chaplains to forty dollars a month;[22] but, to Washington's disappointment, it substituted chaplaincies at the brigade level for the regimental chaplaincies. Washington wanted each regiment to have its own chaplain and to the very end he insisted that "no Establishment appears so good . . . as the Old One."[23]

One of the primary functions of the chaplains was, of course, to conduct services for the soldiers on Sunday. Washington issued the first of many orders regarding Sunday worship two days after his arrival in Cambridge. "The General . . . ," he announced, "requires and expects, of all Officers and Soldiers, not engaged on actual duty, a punctual attendance on divine Service to implore the blessings of heaven upon the means used for our safety and defence."[24] Thereafter, throughout the Revolutionary War, he insisted that his men attend services held by the chaplains on Sunday morning whenever the war situation permitted. "The Commander in Chief," he said, in a typical Sunday service order,

expects an exact compliance with this order, and that it be observed in future as an invariable rule of practice—And every neglect will be considered not only a breach of orders, but a disregard to decency, virtue and religion.[25]

In Washington's opinion, the "regularity and decorum" with which Sunday was observed

will reflect great credit on the army in general, tend to improve the morals, and at the same time, to increase the happiness of the soldiery, and must afford the most pure and rational entertainment for every serious and well disposed mind.[26]

It would also, he hoped, reduce "profane cursing, swearing and drunkenness" in the army.[27]

In addition to Sunday services, Washington from time to time ordered the observance of special days of "Fasting,

Humiliation and Prayer," in compliance with resolutions passed in the Continental Congress. "The General," he declared in one such order,

commands all officers, and soldiers, to pay strict obedience to the Orders of the Continental Congress, and by their unfeigned and pious observance of their religious duties, incline the Lord, and Giver of Victory, to prosper our arms.[28]

There were also days of thanksgiving decreed by Congress, which Washington usually proclaimed in the following fashion:

To morrow being the day set apart by the Honorable Congress for public Thanksgiving and Praise; and duty calling us devoutely to express our grateful acknowledgments to God for the manifold blessings he has granted us. The General directs that the army remain in it's present quarters, and that the Chaplains perform divine service with their several Corps and brigades. And earnestly exhorts, all officers and soldiers, whose absence is not indispensibly necessary, to attend with reverence the solemnities of the day.[29]

Several times during the Revolution, moreover, Washington ordered special thanksgiving services on his own, without any prompting from Congress. In reporting General Horatio Gates's victory over Burgoyne at Saratoga in October, 1777, he declared:

Let every face brighten, and every heart expand with grateful Joy and praise to the supreme disposer of all events, who has granted us this signal success. The Chaplains of the army are to prepare short discourses, suited to the joyful occasion to deliver to their several corps and brigades at 5 O'clock this afternoon. . . .[30]

The conclusion of an alliance with France produced this order on May 5, 1778:

It having pleased the Almighty ruler of the Universe propitiously to defend the Cause of the United American-States and finally by raising us up a powerful Friend among the Princes of the Earth to establish our liberty and Independence up[on] lasting foundations, it becomes us to set apart a day for gratefully acknowledging the divine Goodness and celebrating the important Event which we owe to his benign Interposition.[31]

And on October 20, 1781, following the victory at Yorktown, Washington announced:

Divine Service is to be performed tomorrow in the several Brigades or Divisions.

The Commander in Chief earnestly recommends that the troops not on duty should universally attend with that seriousness of Deportment and gratitude of Heart which the recognition of such reiterated and astonishing interpositions of Providence demand of us.[32]

But religious exhortations of this kind were not confined to orders regarding divine worship; they also appeared in many of Washington's daily orders to his men. An order regarding discipline put it this way on February 27, 1776: "Next to the favour of divine providence, nothing is more essentially necessary to give this Army the victory over all its enemies, than Exactness of discipline, Alertness when on duty, and Cleanliness in their arms and persons...."[33] When announcing a reorganization of his forces following a series of promotions, Washington declared on August 12, 1776:

Under this disposition, formed as well as times will allow, the united efforts of the officers, of every Rank, and the Soldiers, with the smiles of Providence, The General hopes to render a favourable account to his Country, and Posterity of the enemy, whenever they chuse to make the appeal to the great Arbiter of the universe.[34]

In denouncing the "foolish, and wicked practice, of profane cursing and swearing" on August 3, he urged his men to "reflect, that we can have little hopes of the blessing of Heaven on our arms, if we insult it by our impiety and folly. . . ."[35]

Increasingly, as the war continued, Washington seems to have felt that Providence was playing a major role in the progress of the American cause. There were frequent appeals to the Almighty for assistance on the eve of battle, as well as expressions of gratitude for the "remarkable inter- positions of Providence" on behalf of American arms.[36] The surrender of Montreal to American forces in Canada brought this order on November 28, 1775:

The General hopes such frequent Favors from divine provi- dence will animate every American to continue, to exert his utmost, in the defense of the Liberties of his Country, as it would now be basest ingratitude to the Almighty, and to their Country, to shew any the least backwardness in the public cause.[37]

In alerting his men for an engagement with the British in New York, Washington reminded them on June 30, 1776, that "to be well prepared for an engagement is, under God (whose divine Aid it behoves us to supplicate) more than one half the battle."[38] At the end of a similar order on July 2, he declared: "Let us therefore rely upon the goodness of the Cause, and the aid of the Supreme Being, in whose hand Victory is, to animate and encourage us to great and noble Actions. . . ."[39]

An order issued from his headquarters near Germantown on September 13, 1777, commended the soldiers for their "brave fight" on September 11 and added, "he has full confidence that in another Appeal to Heaven with the blessing of providence, which it becomes every officer and soldier humbly to supplicate), we shall prove successful."[40] The news of Benedict Arnold's treason brought this comment in an order of September 26, 1780: "Happily the treason has been timely discovered to prevent the fatal misfortune. The providential train of circumstances which led to it afford the most convincing proof that the Liberties of America are the object of divine Protection."[41]

A preliminary treaty of peace was signed with Great Britain on November 30, 1782, and ratified by Congress on April 15, 1783. In his general orders for April 18, issued from his headquarters at Newburgh, New York, Washington congratulated his men for the "glorious task" which they had accomplished "under the Smiles of Providence" and directed that

the Cessation of Hostilities between the United States of America and the King of Great Britain . . . be publickly proclaimed tomorrow at 12 o'clock [the anniversary of the Battle of Lexington and Concord] at the Newbuilding, and that the Proclamation which will be communicated herewith, be read tomorrow evening at the head of every regiment and corps of the army. After which the Chaplains with the several Brigades will render thanks to almighty God for all his mercies, particularly for his over ruling the wrath of man to his own glory, and causing the rage of war to cease among the nations.[42]

The end of the war was followed inevitably by a series of congratulatory messages to Washington from cities, towns, colleges, churches, and fraternal organizations of various kinds. In acknowledging their compliments, Washington invariably ascribed victory to the "Smiles of Providence" as well as to the efforts of the American people, the valor of the Continental soldiers, and the assistance of France. "I attribute all glory," he said in one such statement,

to that Supreme Being, who hath caused the several parts, which have been employed in the production of the wonderful Events we now contemplate, to harmonize in the most perfect manner, and who was able by the humblest instruments as well as by the most powerful means to establish and secure the liberty and happiness of these United States.[43]

In his farewell orders to the army on November 2, 1783, Washington again declared that the "singular interposition of Providence in our feeble condition were such, as could scarcely escape the attention of the most unobserving. . . ."[44] He then offered "his prayers to the God of Armies" for his men and concluded:

May ample justice be done them here, and may the choicest of heaven's favours, both here and hereafter, attend those who, under the devine auspices, have secured innumerable blessings for others; with these wishes, and this benediction, the Commander in Chief is about to retire from Service. The Curtain of separation will soon be drawn, and the military scene to him will be closed forever.[45]

Washington resigned his commission in a special ceremony before Congress, sitting in Annapolis, on December 23. After listening quietly to a speech by the President of Con-

gress praising him for his great services to the Revolutionary
cause, Washington responded with a brief formal statement
of his own, at the end of which he declared that a

diffidence in my abilities to accomplish so arduous a task . . . was
superseded by a confidence in the rectitude of our Cause, and
the support of the Supreme Power of the Union, and the patronage of Heaven.

The successful Termination of the War has verified the most
sanguine expectations, and my gratitude for the interposition of
Providence, and the assistance I have received from my Countrymen encreases with every review of the momentous Contest.[46]

Probably nothing about Washington has pleased the
pietists as much as the religiosity of many of his orders
and public statements during the American Revolution. "Is
it too much to say," asked William Meade, "that the communications of no king, ruler, general, or statesman in Christendom ever so abounded in expressions of pious dependence
on God?"[47] In claiming Washington as their own, the pietists
have sometimes made almost as much use of his references to
religion during the Revolution as they have of the popular
stories about his piety. "As a military commander," declared
B. F. Morris, with no little justification, "Washington constantly and devoutly acknowledged the special interposition
of a Divine Providence throughout the entire war, and
habitually ascribed the victories and the final results to
God's intervention and goodness. . . ."[48]

True, most of Washington's public statements, as well
as the many orders he issued as Commander in Chief of
the Continental Army, were prepared with the assistance
of members of his staff—Joseph Reed, Tench Tilghman,
David Cobb, Jonathan Trumbull, Jr., David Humphreys,

and others. But like the Farewell Address, they were prepared under Washington's guidance and direction and subject to his revision and final approval. Some of the orders sent
out under his name were probably expressed with more
positive religious feeling than Washington himself habitually
displayed. But none of them was inconsonant with his conviction that religion was one of the "firmest props of the
duties of Men & citizens" and important for the well-being
of his soldiers.[49]

That Washington's Revolutionary orders can also be
regarded as "the brightest evidences of his Christian faith
and piety"—as B. F. Morris went on to assert—is, however,
extremely doubtful.[50] Most of Washington's official communications during the Revolution contained no references
to the Christian religion itself. The appeal, as we have seen,
was customarily made to "Heaven," "Providence," "Supreme
Being," "supreme disposer of all events," and to "the great
arbiter of the Universe." All of these were, of course, expressions that a good Deist—like Thomas Paine, for instance—
could use in all sincerity without in any way committing
himself to the theology and doctrines of the Christian church.

Washington's official policy toward religion as President
of the United States did not differ in essentials from that
which he followed as Revolutionary commander. He was
friendly to—indeed at times he warmly encouraged—organized religion and on more than one public occasion acknowledged his belief in its importance for the life of the new
nation. While he carefully refrained from placing any of his
presidential pronouncements having to do with religion
specifically in a Christian context, he continued to assert,
as he had done during the Revolution, his belief that the

"smiles of Providence" were essential for the peace, prosperity, and happiness of the American people.

In his first inaugural address (which he wrote himself
with perhaps some assistance from James Madison) he
went farther, in fact, than he had ever gone before in
stressing the role of Providence in American affairs. The
second paragraph of his address was devoted almost entirely
to this theme:

> . . . it would be peculiarly improper to omit in this first official
> Act, my fervent supplications to that Almighty Being who rules
> over the Universe, who presides in the Councils of Nations, and
> whose providential aids can supply every human defect, that
> his benediction may consecrate to the liberties and happiness
> of the People of the United States, a Government instituted by
> themselves for these essential purposes: and may enable every
> instrument employed in its administration to execute with suc-
> cess, the functions allotted to his charge. In tendering this
> homage to the Great Author of every public and private good,
> I assure myself that it expresses your sentiments not less than
> my own; nor those of my fellow-citizens at large, less than either.
> No People can be bound to acknowledge and adore the invisible
> hand, which conducts the Affairs of men more than the People
> of the United States. Every step, by which they have advanced
> to the character of an independent nation, seems to have been
> distinguished by some token of providential agency. And in the
> important revolution just accomplished in the system of their
> United Government, the tranquil deliberations and voluntary
> consent of so many distinct communities, from which the event
> has resulted, cannot be compared with the means by which most
> Governments have been established, without some return of
> pious gratitude along with an humble anticipation of the future
> blessings which the past seem to presage. . . .[51]

Thereafter, throughout his presidency, there were
repeated references, in Washington's annual messages to

Congress and in his letters and addresses to state legislatures, city officials, colleges, churches, and fraternal groups, to what he called the "providential agency" in the affairs of the American republic. In his public papers Washington rarely omitted his customary invocation, however brief, of "Divine Providence," "the Supreme Ruler of Nations," "the Author of all good," "the supreme arbiter of events," "the beneficent Being," the "Sovereign Dispenser of life and health," or the "Supreme Architect of the Universe."

On two occasions, moreover, while he was President, Washington issued thanksgiving proclamations (similar to those he had issued to the army during the Revolution) calling upon "all religious societies and denominations, and . . . all persons whomsoever" to set aside special days for giving thanks "to the Great Ruler of Nations for the manifold and signal mercies which distinguish our lot as a nation."[52] The first such proclamation, commemorating the adoption of the Constitution, was given to the public on October 3, 1789, following a resolution passed almost unanimously in the first Congress:

Whereas it is the duty of all Nations to acknowledge the providence of Almighty God, to obey his will, to be grateful for his benefits, and humbly to implore his protection and favor. . . .

Now therefore do I recommend and assign Thursday the 26th. day of November next to be devoted by the People of these States to the service of that great and glorious Being, who is the beneficent Author of all good that was, that is, or that will be.[53]

And so on, for three paragraphs, all of them "breathing," as Anson Phelps Stokes has remarked, "a deeply religious spirit."[54] This first national thanksgiving proclamation under the Constitution had been written by William Jackson, one of Washington's secretaries, and approved by Washington with only one minor revision.[55]

There was some objection in Congress to the proclamation. Thomas Tucker of South Carolina, in particular, opposed having the federal government sponsor a religious observance of this nature. "Why should the President direct the people to do what, perhaps they had no mind to do?" he asked. It was, he insisted, "a business with which Congress has nothing to do; it is a religious matter, and as such is proscribed to us."[56] But Tucker's scruples about the constitutionality of the procedure were not shared by the majority of his colleagues in Congress; and Washington —unlike Thomas Jefferson and Andrew Jackson, who firmly resisted all pressures to proclaim thanksgiving observances of a religious nature while they were Presidents—followed out the congressional recommendation without any apparent personal reservations.[57]

The second proclamation, drafted by Alexander Hamilton and published on January 1, 1795, set aside February 19 as a day of "public thanksgiving and prayer" to celebrate the improvement in the nation's foreign relations and the ending of the Whiskey Insurrection. In addition to urging the American people to express their "affectionate gratitude ... to Almighty God" for these developments, the proclamation also asked them to

beseech the kind Author of these blessings ... to render this country more and more a safe and propitious asylum for the unfortunate of other countries; to extend among us true and useful knowledge; to diffuse and establish habits of sobriety, order, morality, and piety, and, finally, to impart all the blessings we possess, or ask for ourselves to the whole family of mankind.[58]

Washington's thanksgiving proclamations, together with the invocations of the Deity appearing in his presidential addresses, have been regarded by church people as incontrovertible evidence of his Christian orthodoxy. It is necessary to remind ourselves again, however, that his public references to religion while he was President—as during the American Revolution—were invariably phrased in general terms. They could apply to all faiths, non-Christian as well as Christian. Expressions like "Redeemer of the World," "the grace of His Holy Spirit," and "The Great Mediator and Redeemer," which appeared in his successor John Adams' thanksgiving proclamations, were conspicuously absent from Washington's.[59]

Washington's cordiality toward organized religion cannot, of course, be questioned. His concern for the work of chaplains in the army, his orders regarding Sunday services during the Revolution, and the religious allusions appearing in his presidential statements and proclamations show clearly that he looked upon religious precepts and practices as important stabilizing factors in the social life of the American people. He regarded them, as he asserted in his Farewell Address, as fundamental supports for public felicity. While his own behavior as a church member can scarcely be considered orthodox, his views on the social uses of institutional religion were surely conventional enough to satisfy most religionists.

But did religion mean anything more to Washington than this? Did his interest in it transcend his solicitude for social order and for the public happiness? Did it have any meaning for him as an individual? How did he relate it to his own life? And what, in particular, was his attitude toward Christianity? If we are to understand Washington's religion thoroughly, we must know something more about him than his activities as a churchman and his official relations with organized religion as Continental Commander and as President. It is necessary, first, to take up the controversial question as to whether Washington, strictly speaking, can be regarded as a Christian, and, second, to examine his own personal religious philosophy as it appears in his private, as distinguished from his public, papers.

IV

WASHINGTON
AND CHRISTIANITY

IN A BIOGRAPHY of Washington published in 1922, William Roscoe Thayer tells of a little boy who, having listened patiently to a solemn recital of the cherry tree story, exclaimed with some exasperation: "Why couldn't George Washington lie? Couldn't he talk?"[1] The fact is that there were many things—especially those of a highly personal nature—about which Washington couldn't, or wouldn't, talk freely. And, almost invariably, when he might have been tempted to dissemble, he preferred to keep his silence.

"I knew no man," Bishop William White once wrote,

who seemed so carefully to guard against the discoursing of himself or of his acts, or of any thing pertaining to him; and it has occasionally occurred to me, when in his company, that if a stranger to his person were present, he would never have known, from any thing said by the President, that he was conscious of having distinguished himself in the eyes of the world. His ordinary behaviour, although unexceptionably courteous, was not such as to encourage intrusion on what might be in his mind.[2]

Bishop White was thinking particularly of Washington's religious views when he made this comment; and, indeed, when it came to religion, Washington was, if anything, more reserved than he was about anything else pertaining to his life. As Samuel Miller, one of the ministers of the United Presbyterian Church in New York City during Washington's presidency, regretfully observed, Washington habitually displayed an "unusual, but uniform, and apparently deliberate, reticence on the subject of personal religion."[3] It is hardly a matter for surprise that his attitude toward Christianity has been the subject of repeated misunderstanding and apparently endless dispute.

Washington's earliest biographers—even those who refused to place any credence in Parson Weems's imaginative little improvisations about Washington's piety—assumed, without laboring the point, that Washington was a Christian. Aaron Bancroft (1807) declared simply that Washington was Christian in "principle and practice,"[4] and John Marshall (1804-7) said briefly: "Without making ostentatious professions of religion, he was a sincere believer in the Christian faith, and a truly devout man."[5] The doubts raised by Robert Dale Owen and Frances Wright in the 1830's seem to have had little immediate effect on biographers. Jared Sparks (1837) and Washington Irving (1855-59), while making no use of Weems's sentimentalities as source material for describing Washington's religious life, also regarded his Christianity as unquestioned.[6]

In the 1880's, John E. Remsburg, a militant freethinker associated with Robert Green Ingersoll, revived the Owen-

Wright line. In articles and books and on the lecture platform, he punctured the pious myths about Washington with
great zest. It cannot be said, however, that his impact on
Washington biographers was great.[7] With varying degrees
of sophistication, such writers as Henry Cabot Lodge
(1889), Woodrow Wilson (1896), Sir George Otto Trevel-
yan (1915), William Roscoe Thayer (1922), Luther A.
Weigle (1928), and John C. Fitzpatrick (1931) believed
that Washington could in some sense be characterized as
a Christian.[8] Rupert Hughes (1926-30) was one of the few
twentieth-century biographers to attack with vigor certain
of the traditional legends about Washington's orthodoxy,
but he did not make an exhaustive study of Washington's
religion.[9] More recently, Douglas Southall Freeman treated
Washington's religion with his customary caution and candor, but he did not make it a primary subject of his concern
as a biographer.[10] Much, in fact, remains to be said about
Washington's relation to the Christian religion.

Secular freethinkers, reacting against the exuberances of
the pietists, have been fond of pointing out that in all of
Washington's voluminous writings there does not appear
even a single reference to Jesus Christ. They are in error;
there is one such reference. In a speech to the Delaware
Chiefs at Washington's Middle Brook headquarters on May
12, 1779 (which the pietists have unaccountably overlooked), appears this passage: "You will do well to wish to
learn our ways of life, and above all, the religion of Jesus
Christ. These will make you a greater and happier people
than you are." But this speech, like many of Washington's
speeches during the Revolutionary period, was probably
written by one of his aides, Robert Hanson Harrison, and

Washington, who must have been pressed for time, seems simply to have signed the document without making any revisions.[11] On a later occasion, some years afterward, he was more careful—or more tactful—in dealing with the Indians. In the draft of a speech to some Indian leaders which had been prepared for him by a clerk in the War Department he took the trouble to cross out the word "God" and substitute the expression "the Great Spirit above."[12]

From time to time, general references to Christianity do appear in Washington's writings. But even in his public statements they are remarkably few. In his general orders regarding chaplains on July 9, 1776, appears this sentence: "The General hopes and trusts, that every officer and man, will endeavour so to live, and act, as becomes a Christian soldier defending the dearest Rights and Liberties of his country."[13] And one of his orders regarding Sunday services in the army declared on May 2, 1778:

While we are zealously performing the duties of good Citizens and soldiers we certainly ought not to be inattentive to the higher duties of Religion. To the distinguished Character of Patriot, it should be our highest Glory to add the more distinguished Character of Christian.[14]

Christian writers have set great store by these passages, one of them remarking with immense satisfaction that Washington coined the expression "Christian soldiers" long before Rev. Sabine Baring-Gould composed the hymn, "Onward, Christian Soldiers."[15] But like the speech to the Delaware Indians, these orders were in part the compositions of members of Washington's staff and they reflect simply Washington's determination to utilize the services of chaplains to build morale and discipline in the army. What is noteworthy, as a matter of fact, is that Washington's staff writers, some of them with sincere Christian convictions of their own, made such infrequent use of Christian phraseology in the documents which they prepared for their commander. In this respect they reflected Washington's reserve on the subject almost perfectly.

There is one notable exception: the circular letter which Washington sent to the governors of the thirteen states from his headquarters in Newburgh, New York, a few months after the conclusion of a preliminary peace treaty with Great Britain. It was perhaps the most famous document issued under Washington's signature during the Revolution, and it contained references to the Christian religion which were unusual for Washington. Dated June 8, 1783, it was Washington's last official communication to the states as Continental Commander; and because it outlined at length the political and economic policies deemed indispensable for the well-being of the newly independent nation, it is sometimes called "Washington's Legacy."[16] In one moving passage, the letter described the noble future to which the American people could look forward. The citizens of the United States, Washington declared, "are, from this period, to be considered as the Actors on a most conspicuous Theatre, which seems to be peculiarly designated by Providence for the display of human greatness and felicity." The availability of rich natural resources, together with "the Treasures of knowledge, acquired by the labours of Philosophers, Sages and Legislatures, through a long succession of years," he pointed out, gave "a fairer oppertunity for political happiness, than any other Nation has ever been favored with. . . ." Moreover, the American nation had the great advantage of having been born, not in "the gloomy age of Ignorance and Superstition," but in an age of enlightenment, in which

the free cultivation of letters, the unbounded extension of Commerce, the progressive refinement of Manners, the growing liberality of sentiment, and, above all, the pure and benign light of Revelation, have had a meliorating influence on mankind and increased the blessings of Society.[17]

The reference to "the pure and benign light of Revelation" has naturally been much remarked on by orthodox Christian writers. But the closing paragraph of Washington's "valedictory" has been even more highly treasured. "I now make it my earnest prayer," Washington concluded,

that God would have you, and the State over which you preside, in his holy protection, that he would incline the hearts of the Citizens to cultivate a spirit of subordination and obedience to Government, to entertain a brotherly affection and love for one another, for their fellow Citizens of the United States at large, and particularly for their brethren who have served in the Field, and finally, that he would most graciously be pleased to dispose us all, to do Justice, to love mercy, and to demean ourselves with that Charity, humility, and pacific temper of mind, which were the Characteristicks of the Divine Author of our blessed Religion, and without an humble imitation of whose example in these things, we can never hope to be a happy Nation.[18]

The allusion to "the Divine Author of our blessed Religion" was unmistakably a reference to Jesus Christ, and it has been considered conclusive evidence of Washington's belief in the divinity of Christ. "What more satisfactory evidence," insisted McGuire, "could be asked or given, of unqualified faith in Revelation as a fact, or in the doctrines announced thereby."[19] "Can a man's pen," asked Buffington, "record any clearer statement of his unquestioned belief in the divinity of Christ and that his own life was an humble imitation of that of Christ?"[20] In a controversy over the passage that raged in the *New York Tribune* in 1902, Henry Cabot Lodge declared categorically: "Washington either believed in the divinity of Christ or when he wrote those words he deliberately stated something which he did not believe."[21]

With the words "Almighty God" placed at the beginning of the passage and "Through Jesus Christ Our Lord" at the end, and with some changes in the text, the final paragraph of Washington's circular letter to the thirteen states has been called "Washington's Prayer."[22] In this form it soon received an independent existence of its own, and eventually it was inscribed on a bronze tablet in St. Paul's Chapel in New York City.[23] *The World Almanac* for 1930, in fact, stated that Washington made this "prayer" in St. Paul's following his inauguration as President in April, 1789;[24] and at least one writer also erred in asserting that it was composed by Washington on the occasion of the signing of the Declaration of Independence.[25] In a special ceremony honoring Washington on June 2, 1947, the Board of Governors of the American Bar Association placed a wreath on Washington's tomb at Mount Vernon and then listened to a reading of the "prayer" which, according to the *American Bar Association Journal*, "may well be uttered by men and women in this time."[26]

The use made of the final paragraph in Washington's

circular letter has evoked considerable indignation among freethinkers. Franklin Steiner declared that the letter was written by one of Washington's military secretaries and that in it Washington was merely expressing the hope that some help would come to "the distracted country."[27] Joseph McCabe insisted that the language employed in the so-called "prayer" was language "which many a skeptic in high position has used" and was no indication of Washington's orthodoxy.[28] Rupert Hughes put it this way:

From this long, long document, this argumentative prayer to the unruly colonies and their congresses, the tail has actually been chopped off, dressed up, engrossed, illuminated, distributed and vastly displayed under the name, "Washington's Prayer."

To Hughes, the "distortion of his purpose" was "astonishing," especially in view of the fact that the letter was not even in Washington's handwriting.[29] It is possible, Hughes acknowledged, that Washington "may have dictated it and felt it at the time"; but, he added, "it was an open letter to the governors of the states beseeching their help and not heaven's. . . ."[30]

Whether Washington composed the circular letter himself in its entirety or whether parts of the letter—in particular, the "prayer"—were the work of his staff writers, it is impossible to say on the basis of available information. Douglas Freeman, in his discussion of the document, stated that it had been prepared by Washington and some of his assistants, though he gave no source for his statement.[31] Elsewhere, Freeman gave it as his opinion that some of the official papers issued by Washington during the Revolution were drafted by staff writers who were more devout than Washington and who customarily added religious touches of their own to public statements which they drafted for the Commander in Chief.[32] In the introduction to his collection of Washington's writings, John C. Fitzpatrick (who utilized the copy of the circular letter which was in David Cobb's handwriting)[33] pointed out that during the Revolution drafts of letters going out from headquarters were drawn up by an aide or a secretary from a rough memorandum of Washington's, by Washington's verbal direction, or, in some instances, were written out by Washington himself.[34] But Washington "dominated his correspondence," Fitzpatrick went on to say, "and cannot be denied complete responsibility for it."[35]

This much, certainly, is true: Washington signed the circular letter and sent it out as an expression of his official views. That it embodied his ideas on the agency of Providence in the affairs of the American people (to which he frequently alluded in his private correspondence) and his belief that religion was important for good citizenship is not open to question. But that the specific way in which these sentiments were expressed in the final paragraph of the letter (whether by himself or by one of his staff writers) represented a literal statement of Washington's religious beliefs is more than doubtful. Nowhere else, in any of Washington's writings, public or private, does a similar reference to Jesus Christ appear. Nor does Washington, in speaking of religion, express himself in any other place in language even remotely approaching the language of the closing paragraph of the circular letter of 1783. Unlike Thomas Jefferson —and Thomas Paine, for that matter—Washington never even got around to recording his belief that Christ was a great ethical teacher. His reticence on the subject was truly remarkable.

Washington frequently alluded to Providence in his private correspondence. But the name of Christ, in any connection whatsoever, does not appear anywhere in his many letters to friends and associates throughout his life. Gouverneur Morris once wrote him to say: "Had our Saviour addressed a Chapter to the Rulers of Mankind, I am persuaded his Good Sense would have dictated this Text: Be not wise overmuch."[36] In his reply, Washington avoided speaking of the "Saviour." "Had such a chapter as you speak of," he said, "been written to the rulers of Mankind, it would, I am persuaded, have been as unavailing as many others upon subjects of equal importance."[37]

Dismayed by this massive silence regarding Christ in Washington's writings, J. B. Buckley, writing in 1896, attempted to explain it away by asserting that it "was not then, and is not now the habit of Christian men to mention the name of Christ in correspondence upon general subjects."[38] But it was, in fact, the habit of Washington's contemporary, Dr. Benjamin Rush. Rush, a devout Christian, though without orthodox denominational attachments, was not at all reserved about speaking of the "Son of God," "that holy Jesus," and the "Saviour of the World" in writing to his friends.[39] John Adams and Thomas Jefferson, moreover, discussed "the fundamentals of Jesus's teachings" at some length in letters to one another toward the end of their lives.[40] Jefferson himself (usually regarded as unspeakably heterodox by pietistic writers) took the subject seriously enough to compile "The Philosophy of Jesus of Nazareth" and to prepare a "Syllabus of an Estimate of the Merit of the Doctrines of Jesus, Compared with Those of Others."[41] Even Thomas Paine (whom Theodore Roosevelt once called "a dirty little atheist") declared his opinion that Jesus was "an amiable and virtuous man" and that the "morality that he preached and practiced was of the most benevolent kind. . . ."[42] But nowhere in Washington's letters does there appear a humanistic reference, direct or implied, to Jesus and his teachings.

Only rarely, furthermore, in his private letters, did Washington say anything about the Christian religion in general. And when he did, he said nothing that would throw any light on his opinions about Christian doctrines. A letter to Major General Israel Putnam on October 19, 1777, on the occasion of Mrs. Putnam's death, for example, declared, among other things: "I hope you will bear the misfortune with that fortitude and complacency of mind, that become a man and a Christian."[43] In another letter, dated December 23, 1793, in which he remonstrated with John Christian Ehler, his gardener at Mount Vernon, for drunkenness, Washington declared: "Shew yourself more of a man, and a Christian, than to yield to so intolerable a vice. . . ."[44] There are also general references to Christianity in letters to the Countess of Huntingdon, a devout Methodist who wrote from England to propose a plan for propagating the gospel among the Western Indians,[45] and to John Ettwein, active in the Moravian Society for Propagating the Gospel among the Heathen.[46] To both, Washington cordially expressed his approbation of efforts to convert the Indians "to Christianity and consequently to civilization," but it is difficult to see how one can draw any conclusions regarding Christian doctrine from these sentiments.[47]

During the Revolution and while he was President, Washington was the recipient of numerous sermons, printed in pamphlet form, which had been delivered by clergymen of various denominations on special occasions—fast days, days of thanksgiving, Fourth of July, and the like—and he always responded with a polite note of acknowledgment to the authors. But we know little of what Washington thought of these sermons. Probably he did not get around to reading most of them. In his acknowledgments, he sometimes merely said that he looked forward to "perusing" the sermon in question.[48] If the sermon had been dedicated to him—and many were—he thanked the clergyman for so honoring him;[49] and if, as often happened, the sermon contained complimentary references to his public services, he expressed appreciation for the "favourable sentiments" voiced by the author.[50] But only rarely did he comment on the substance of the sermon, and these infrequent comments provide us with little insight into his attitude toward Christian doctrines.

In March, 1778, for example, he wrote Rev. Israel Evans, brigade chaplain for the New Hampshire troops, to thank him for sending a copy of a discourse which Evans had preached on December 18, 1777, a day set apart by Congress for a general thanksgiving. The text of the sermon was Psalm 115, beginning, "Not unto us, O Lord, not unto us, but unto thy name give glory." The sermon was filled with praise for Washington's character and ability, and at one point Evans exclaimed: "Oh! Americans, give glory to God for such a faithful hero!" Then, after hailing the recent victory at Saratoga, Evans closed his sermon by exhorting "to fidelity and sacrifice the lives of true Christians."[51] In his letter to Evans, Washington said that he had read the sermon "with attention and pleasure";[52] he could scarcely have done otherwise. He expressed similar satisfaction with a thanksgiving sermon delivered by Jedidiah Morse, Congregational minister, staunch Federalist, and "father of American geography," to celebrate the passing of the French crisis in 1798. But what Washington particularly liked was the appendix which Morse had added to the sermon, "exhibiting proofs of the early existence, progress and deleterious effects of French intrigue and influence in the United States."[53] Washington told Morse that he had read the appendix "with pleasure" and wished that it "could meet a more general circulation" because it contained "important information."[54] What he thought of the sermon itself he did not say.

In only two instances did Washington express his opinion on the content of sermons which had been forwarded to him. In August, 1797, when he received a collection of sermons from Rev. Zechariah Lewis, twenty-four-year-old tutor at Yale College, he wrote to say: "The doctrine in them is sound, and does credit to the Author."[55] Unfortunately, we do not know whose sermons they were (they were not Lewis', for the young tutor had published nothing at this time), and consequently we have no way of knowing what the doctrine was that Washington considered "sound."

In the second instance, however, we can speak with some precision. In 1789, a few months after Washington's inauguration, Rev. Joseph Buckmaster of New Hampshire sent the new President a sermon which presumably might be of particular interest to Washington as he assumed the highest office in the new federal government. It was an old sermon. It had been preached by Benjamin Stevens, pastor of the first church in Kittery, Maine, on the occasion of the death of Sir William Pepperell in 1759, and had been printed as a pamphlet in Boston during the same year.[56] Pepperell had been an important figure in colonial New England, as a merchant, as president of the Massachusetts Council, and as head of the Maine militia and commander of the expedition which captured Louisbourg, French stronghold on Cape Breton, in 1744. Stevens' funeral sermon took Psalm 82:7 as its text—"But ye shall die like Men"—and it stressed the point that "the highest in Dignity and Station are not exempted any more than the lowest from the impartial Stroke of Death."[57] It was the will of God, asserted Stevens, that men should live under some form of civil authority and "in this Sense civil Rulers *are of God* and his *Establishment and Appointment.*" They should, therefore, be accorded great respect because of their "Power and Usefulness" and they may even, as the preceding verses in Psalms indicated, "without Impropriety be stiled *Gods.*"[58] But they should never be idolized for they are "but *Men,* —the same feeble, frail Creatures that all the Sons of Men are" and "according to the natural Course of Things they must die as well as others. . . ."[59] The "Great as well as the Small," Stevens emphasized, "are to stand before the tribunal of the universal Judge; they shall be judged in like Manner without Respect of Persons, and receive according to the Deeds done in the Body."[60] His conclusion: the "universal Reign of Death" should teach the "most exalted in Station" to consider "the Duties rather than the Dignity of . . . Station, to discharge every Trust with Diligence and Fidelity, and to improve every Talent to the Acceptance of the great Lord and Proprietor. . . ."[61] In acknowledging receipt of this sermon, Washington voiced his hearty "approbation of the doctrine therein inculcated."[62] Whether it was the humility or the conscientiousness enjoined upon men in high office that appealed to Washington we have no way of knowing. Probably it was both. In any case, the doctrine which he approved was primarily of political significance and does not enlighten us as to his attitude toward the tenets of the Christian faith.

In 1795, Rev. Uzal Ogden sent Washington a copy of his two-volume treatise, *Antidote to Deism*, a refutation of Paine's *Age of Reason*, which he had dedicated to Washington without the latter's permission. Ogden told Washington that he had written it "to check the Progress of Infidelity" in the United States, and he added: "I shall be happy if the work shall be honored with your approbation." A letter of endorsement by Washington would, of course, have been widely publicized. But no reply to Ogden has been found in the Washington papers. As Samuel Eliot Morison put it, Washington "refused to bite" on this occasion.[63]

On another and more famous occasion, Washington also seems to have refused to "bite." Thomas Jefferson recorded the episode in an entry for February 1, 1800, in the journal which he called the *Anas*:

Dr. Rush tells me that he had it from Asa Green that when the clergy addressed Genl. Washington on his departure from the govmt., it was observed in their consultation that he had never on any occasion said a word to the public which showed a belief in the Xn religion and they thot they should so pen their address as to force him at length to declare publicly whether he was a Christian or not. They did so. However he observed the old fox was too cunning for them. He answered every article of

their address particularly except that, which he passed over
without notice.[64]

So frequently has this passage been cited by freethinkers
as evidence of Washington's anticlerical bent, as well as
his lack of Christian orthodoxy, that the entire episode
to which Jefferson referred somewhat vaguely is worth
examining with some care.[65]

The Dr. Rush to whom Jefferson referred was, of course,
Benjamin Rush, the famous Philadelphia physician.[66] The
Asa Green mentioned by Jefferson was Ashbel Green (1762-
1848), one of the ministers of the Second Presbyterian
Church in Philadelphia, chaplain in the House of Representatives during Washington's presidency, and later president
of the College of New Jersey.[67]

The address on the occasion of Washington's retirement
from office, to which Jefferson had reference, was dated
March 3, 1797, signed by twenty-four clergymen of various
Protestant denominations in the Philadelphia area, including
Ashbel Green, and was read in person to Washington by
Bishop William White, first Protestant Episcopal bishop of
the diocese of Pennsylvania, with the other signers present.
Consisting of four paragraphs, the address, after com-
mending Washington for his many years of public service,
declared (in its sole reference to Christianity) that "in our
special character as ministers of the gospel of Christ, we
are more immediately bound to acknowledge the countenance which you have uniformly given to his holy religion."
Then followed the bulk of the address: a passage from
Washington's Farewell Address calling religion and morality
"indispensable supports" of political and social order, followed by a warm endorsement by the clergymen of the

"just and pious sentiments" expressed by the President in his valedictory to the nation.[68]

In his response, Washington reiterated his belief that *"Religion* and *Morality* are the essential pillars of civil society" and then shifted to his favorite topic when making addresses before church groups: religious toleration. "I view," he said,

with unspeakable pleasure, that harmony and Brotherly Love which characterizes the clergymen of different denominations— as well in this, as in other parts of the United States; exhibiting to the world a new and interesting spectacle, at once the pride of our Country and the surest basis of universal Harmony.

He concluded by calling on the "Divine Author of life and felicity" to crown the clergymen's "Labours for the good of Mankind" with success.[69] How much smoking out on the part of the Philadelphia clergymen and of tactful evasion on Washington's part was there in all of this?

Writing many years after the event, Arthur B. Bradford, a Presbyterian minister and an associate of Green's in the Philadelphia presbytery and later consul in Amoy, China, during Abraham Lincoln's first administration,[70] declared that Green

often said in my hearing, though very sorrowfully, of course, that while Washington was very deferential to religion and its ceremonies, like nearly all the founders of the Republic, he was not a Christian, but a Deist.[71]

Moreover, according to Bradford, Green once

explained more at length the plan laid by the clergy of Philadelphia at the close of Washington's administration to get his views of religion for the sake of the good influence they supposed they would have in counteracting the Infidelity of Paine and the rest of the Revolutionary patriots, military and civil. But I well remember the smile on his face and the twinkle of his black eyes when he said: "The old fox was too cunning for us."[72]

In an extended comment on the passage in Jefferson's *Anas* written in 1830, however, Ashbel Green took sharp exception to Jefferson's (and, by implication, Bradford's) version of the exchange. According to Green, on March 1, 1797, three days before Washington stepped down from office, the clergymen of different denominations in the city and vicinity of Philadelphia held a meeting to draw up the congratulatory address. At this meeting, a committee of three, composed of Bishop White, William Smith (Anglican clergyman and first provost of the College of Philadelphia), and Green himself, was appointed to draft the document. Green "penned" the address, he recalled, in its entirety, and it was accepted by the committee and by the clergymen as a whole without any fundamental alterations. On March 2, Green continued, the committee waited on Washington and furnished him with a copy of the address so that he could prepare a suitable reply. The following day, the clergymen called on Washington in a body, presented him with the draft of the address which had been prepared by Green, and received his answer.[73]

In all of the "consultations of the clergy," Green insisted, not a "single syllable" was uttered regarding Washington's failure to state publicly his commitment to the Christian faith. Any such "allegation," declared Green, would have been "palpably false," since, in his opinion, there was never any doubt as to Washington's orthodoxy. Bishop White, moreover, Green went on to say, "has assured us, that he has no trace of recollection that anything was said in the two meetings of the clergy, relative to the neglect of the President to declare his belief on the subject of divine revelation...."[74] The contents of the address itself, finally, Green emphasized, reveal that there was no intention of forcing Washington to declare whether he was a Christian or not.[75]

And yet, having said all of this in refutation of Jefferson's report of the episode, Green then proceeded to make substantial concessions in the direction of the Jefferson version. "It is also true," he acknowledged,

that in penning the address, it was in the mind of the writer (he knows not that it was in any other mind) that a full and fair opportunity should be given him to speak, on leaving the chair of state, as he had spoken on quitting his military command, and that the address was framed with some reference to this subject.[76]

The statement made by Washington "on quitting his military command" which Green had in mind was also mentioned by Jefferson in the *Anas*. After describing Washington's encounter with the Philadelphia clergymen, Jefferson added:

Rush observed he never did say a word on the subject in any of his public papers except in his valedictory to the Governors of the states when he resigned his commission, wherein he speaks of the benign influence of the Christian religion.[77]

Both Green and Jefferson were referring, of course, to the circular letter of 1783, which was issued some months before Washington actually resigned his military commission. Like all orthodox believers, Green derived great satisfaction from the reference to "the pure and benign light of Revelation" and from the concluding paragraph of the circular letter, and he obviously hoped that words of a similar nature would be spoken by Washington to the Philadelphia ministers. But, he continued ruefully,

It is in like manner true, that General Washington did not see proper to do what the writer of the address hoped he would do; that the writer, also, regretted this omission, and regrets it still; and that in conversation with his friends he had occasionally mentioned the facts which he now states. He has not, indeed, the slightest recollection of having ever named them to Dr. Rush; but as he had the honor of an intimate acquaintance with that gentleman, he does not question that he repeated the facts to him; and that the Doctor mentioned them in some conversation had with Mr. J.[78]

Nevertheless, Green expressed great indignation over Jefferson's final comment in the *Anas* on Washington's religion. "I know," Jefferson had written, in concluding his entry, "that Gouverneur Morris, who pretended to be in his secrets & believed himself to be so, has often told me that Genl. Washington believed no more of that system than he himself did."[79] Washington, retorted Green, was in no sense an "infidel," as Jefferson implied.

The writer of the address most assuredly never did think, or say, that General Washington was an infidel; but he has said, and he says now, that it would have given him gratification, if that great man had thought proper, during his presidency, or at its close, to speak out *again*, as he had once spoken before—spoken in such a manner as not to permit the enemies of revealed truth to use even his silence, for the vile purposes for which they now endeavour to employ it. What were the considerations which induced him to be reserved on the subject, we know not. . . . Perhaps he thought that this was going as far as the proprieties of his station, in the peculiar circumstances in which he was placed, required or permitted him to go. Nor are we unapprized that there are men, of whose belief of Christianity no doubt exists, who think that President Washington acted, in the matter here contemplated, exactly right; and that it must be attributed to our clerical views and feelings that we should wish him to have gone farther. Be it so—We do wish he had gone farther.[80]

To the unbiased observer, then, the Jefferson-Bradford version of the affair seems to have been, in the main, accurate. By his own admission, Green did wish Washington to commit himself publicly to the Christian religion; he did frame the congratulatory address with this in mind; and he did regret that Washington failed to rise to the occasion. Jefferson (or perhaps Rush) seems to have erred only in supposing that it was the clergymen as a whole, rather than Green himself, who were trying to elicit a confession of faith from the President. It can scarcely be considered an egregious error.

One can only guess at the reasons that prompted Washington to omit even a brief and noncommital reference to Christianity in his response to Green's address. Possibly he sensed Green's purpose, as Jefferson was led to believe, and, somewhat annoyed by the attempted intrusion upon his privacy, studiously avoided seizing the bait. Only the day before, in replying to an address of the rector, churchwardens, and vestrymen of the United Episcopal Churches of Christ and St. Peter's, he had been willing, as we have seen, to speak of his personal gratification for the "liberal and interesting discourses which have been delivered in your Churches."

On the other hand, the impersonal nature of his response to Green's address may not have been deliberate. Washington had many exchanges with religious groups while he was President, and he rarely made any mention of Christianity in his remarks. In a letter to the General Assembly of the Presbyterian Church in May, 1789, it is true, he declared that "no man, who is profligate in his morals, or a bad member of the civil community, can possibly be a true Christian, or a credit to his own religious society."[81] He also referred to "pious Christians" in a communication to the Synod of the Dutch Reformed Church in October, 1789,[82] and to "the pure spirit of Christianity" in an address to American Catholics in March, 1790.[83] But, with these exceptions, Washington's practice was to speak of religion in only the most general terms when exchanging felicities with church groups during his presidency.

There is a myth (and it was revived in 1962 during the discussion following the Supreme Court's decision against the constitutionality of state-sponsored prayers in public schools) to the effect that Washington once declared while he was President that the government of the United States "is not in any sense founded on the Christian religion." But the statement was not Washington's; it was Joel Barlow's, and it appeared in the Treaty of Peace and Friendship which Barlow, American consul in Algiers, concluded with Tripoli on November 4, 1796. Eager to make it clear that Christianity was not an American state religion and that therefore the United States government bore no official hostility toward Mohammedanism, Barlow declared in Article XI of the treaty:

As the Government of the United States of America is not in any sense founded on the Christian religion; as it has in itself no character of enmity against the laws, religion, or tranquillity of Musselmen; and as the said States never have entered into any war or act of hostility against any Mehomitan nation, it is declared by the parties, that no pretext arising from religious opinions shall ever produce an interruption of the harmony existing between the two countries.[84]

Though negotiated while Washington was President, the treaty was not ratified by the Senate until June, 1797, shortly after John Adams became President; and in 1805, during Jefferson's presidency, it was superseded by a new Treaty of Peace and Amity in which the clause was omitted.[85] The Tripoli treaty, in short, can scarcely be taken as revelatory of Washington's attitude toward Christianity. Very likely Washington shared Barlow's views, though there is no record of his opinion about the treaty; his policy, however, was uniformly one of judicious self-restraint when it came to making public pronouncements about the Christian religion.*

Ashbel Green was not the only contemporary of Washington's who was saddened by the first President's implacable reserve on the subject of Christianity. In a letter to Manasseh Cutler not long after Washington's death, Benjamin Tallmadge expressed great sorrow over the fact that

---

*It may be worth remarking in this connection that that devout seventeenth-century American Puritan, Roger Williams, would undoubtedly, for quite different reasons, have heartily endorsed Barlow's dissociation of the Christian religion from the United States government. Williams, among other things, charged James I of England with blasphemy for having referred to Europe as "Christendom" and as "the Christian world." Christianity meant too much to Williams to be bandied about in such a loose and careless fashion. Twentieth-century crusaders for a "Christian amendment" to the American Constitution might well ponder the case of Williams — as well as that of Barlow and Washington.

the late President had never been "explicit in his profession of *faith in,* and *dependence on* the finished Atonement of our glorious Redeemer...."[86] Rev. Samuel Miller of New York also, it was said,

often spoke, with sadness, of the doubt clouding his own mind as to Washington's piety. How was it possible, he asked, for a true Christian, in the full exercise of his mental faculties, to die without one expression of distinctive belief, or Christian hope....[87]

One is led inescapably to Bishop White's opinion on this much-discussed subject. "I do not believe," White declared many years after Washington's death, when the subject was being aired in public,

that any degree of recollection will bring to my mind any fact which would prove General Washington to have been a believer in the Christian revelation; further than as may be hoped from his constant attendance on Christian worship....[88]

James Madison was probably correct when he told Jared Sparks in 1830 that he did

not suppose that Washington had ever attended to the arguments for Christianity, and for the different systems of religion, or in fact that he had formed definite opinions on the subject. But he took these things as he found them existing, and was constant in his observance of worship according to the received forms of the Episcopal Church in which he was brought up.[89]

If to be a member of a Christian church, to attend church with a fair degree of regularity, to insist on the importance of organized religion for society, and to believe in an over-ruling Providence in human affairs is to be a Christian, then Washington can assuredly be regarded as a Christian. Bird Wilson, in reconsidering his views on Washington's religion, finally decided that these were sufficient to characterize Washington as such. Washington's

aid given for the support of the Church, in his own parish—the correct sentiments on religion contained in several of his public addresses—the unimpeached sincerity of his character, manifested through life, and forbidding a suspicion that those sentiments were not really entertained—and his attendance on the public services of the house of God, furnish satisfactory proof of his respect for religion and of his belief in Christianity....[90]

On the other hand, if to believe in the divinity and resurrection of Christ and his atonement for the sins of man and to participate in the sacrament of the Lord's Supper are requisites for the Christian faith, then Washington, on the evidence which we have examined, can hardly be considered a Christian, except in the most nominal sense. "That Washington was a professing Christian," declared Dr. James Abercrombie,

is evident from his regular attendance in our church; but, Sir, I cannot consider any man as a real Christian who uniformly disregards an ordinance so solemnly enjoined by the divine Author of our holy religion, and considered as a channel of divine grace.[91]

One may indeed define Christianity broadly enough (as it is increasingly defined in the United States today) to include Washington within the fold; but this is to place him at a considerable distance from the kind of Christianity which the pietists are talking about when they claim Washington as one of their own. If Washington was a Christian, he was surely a Protestant of the most liberal persuasion. He was, as Bird Wilson lamented in his Albany sermon, more of a "unitarian" than anything else in his apparent lack of doctrinal convictions.

V

WASHINGTON'S
RELIGIOUS OPINIONS

ON ONE POINT at least Ashbel Green was entirely correct: Washington was no infidel, if by infidel is meant unbeliever. Washington had an unquestioning faith in Providence and, as we have seen, he voiced this faith publicly on numerous occasions. That this was no mere rhetorical flourish on his part, designed for public consumption, is apparent from his constant allusions to Providence in his personal letters. There is every reason to believe, from a careful analysis of religious references in his private correspondence, that Washington's reliance upon a Grand Designer along Deist lines was as deep-seated and meaningful for his life as, say, Ralph Waldo Emerson's serene confidence in a Universal Spirit permeating the ever shifting appearances of the everyday world. Washington's faith was by no means as complex and subtle as Emerson's. As he told James Anderson: "... in politics, as in religion, my tenets are few and simple. ..."[1]

What were Washington's religious tenets? Neither pietist

nor freethinker has taken the trouble to examine them carefully as they appear in letters to his closest friends and colleagues. The pietists have been too busy manufacturing legends and the freethinkers too busy discrediting them to leave much time for finding out what Washington himself had to say. But in his private writings Washington said a good deal, in passing, on the subject of religion, even if he never gathered his thoughts together in an orderly fashion. Twentieth-century scholars customarily lump Washington with Jefferson, Franklin, and Paine as a Deist and let it go at that. But Washington was not a Jefferson or a Franklin or a Paine, and his religious views were by no means identical with theirs. Broadly speaking, of course, Washington can be classified as a Deist. But this is to tell us little of a specific nature about his religious opinions which were, as a matter of fact, somewhat at variance with those of Jefferson, Franklin, and Paine. Instead of letting other people speak for Washington in the area of religion, as has been so often the practice, it seems only fair to let Washington speak for himself, to assume that he meant what he said, and to analyze what he said carefully. No other approach is likely to throw as much light on what has been called the "mystery" of Washington's personality and his innermost thoughts and feelings.

Writing to Ebenezer Hazard on May 2, 1789, Jeremy Belknap declared: "Nothing can add a greater lustre to General Washington than the deep sense of religion which seems to fill his soul. . . ."[2] Belknap undoubtedly exaggerated the profundity of Washington's religious feelings. Still, Washington's faith was real enough. "No man," he once told Rev. William Gordon, "has a more perfect Reliance on the alwise and powerful dispensations of the Supreme Being than I have nor thinks his aid more necessary."[3]

The Supreme Being whose aid he counted upon Washington usually called Providence, Heaven, or, to a lesser extent, God. But he also made much use of such stock Deist phrases as Grand Architect, Governor of the Universe, Higher Cause, Great Ruler of Events, Supreme Architect of the Universe, Author of the Universe, Great Creator, Director of Human Events, and Supreme Ruler. Only rarely did he mention "Fate" or "Fortune" in his writings, and when he did it is clear that he did not regard them as synonyms for Providence. He acknowledged the hand of Providence, for example, in the "Fate of America"[4] and he thanked God for the help he had received as Commander in Chief of the Continental Army "in every vicissitude of Fortune."[5] Moreover, the nature of the supernatural being whose existence he never doubted was quite clear in Washington's mind, as were the relations between this being and the affairs of men.

The Supreme Being was, in the first place, an "Omnipotent Being."[6] It was "powerful to save."[7] In a letter to Martha Custis on July 20, 1758, on the eve of his march to the Ohio, Washington's prayer was that "an all-powerful Providence may keep us both in safety. . . ."[8] Throughout the Revolution he looked confidently to the "Power which has hitherto sustained the American arms"[9] for help in times of crisis, and after the Revolution he frequently expressed his gratitude to that "Power, which hath hitherto kept us from Disunion and Anarchy."[10] Washington believed that human beings must accept the "all powerful decrees" of Providence without protest.[11] But he insisted that its decrees were always for the best and that the "Omnipotent Being" had never "deserted the cause of America in the hour of its extremest hazard. . . ."[12]

The Supreme Being, in the second place, possessed "Infinite Wisdom."[13] It was an "All Wise Creator"[14] who always "wisely orders the Affairs of Men. . . ."[15] While its decrees seem at times "to bear hard upon us," he told his lifelong friend Bryan Fairfax, they are "all ways wise" and are "meant for gracious purposes."[16] In March, 1776, Washington was sorely disappointed when unexpected bad weather prevented him from undertaking an operation he had planned against the British. But, as he wrote both his friend Landon Carter and his brother John Augustine Washington: "That this remarkable interposition of Providence is for some wise purpose, I have no doubt."[17]

Washington admitted that it was difficult at times to be sure of the "divine wisdom" in the ordering of events; but in the end he invariably made the reconciliation.[18] Discussing unrest in Europe with the Marquis de Chastellux in 1785, Washington set forth his own aspirations for a world in peace and harmony and then added: but "a wise providence, I presume, has ordered it otherwise, and we must go on in the old way disputing, and now and then fighting, until the Globe itself is dissolved."[19] He voiced similar misgivings to the Marquis de Lafayette the following year, exclaiming: "Melancholy reflection! For what wise purpose does Providence permit this? Is it as a scourge for mankind, or is it to prevent them from becoming too populous?"[20] Whatever the answer, faith in the ultimate wisdom of the "determinations of Providence" steeled Washington against bitterness and despair in times of trouble.[21] "At disappointments and

losses which are the effects of Providential acts," he told
William Pearce, "I never repine; because I am sure the
divine disposer of events knows better than we do, what
is best for us, or what we deserve."[22] He was thus able to look
with hope and confidence to the future. "Will not the All
Wise and all powerful director of human events, preserve
[America]?" he cried, in the midst of a discussion of the
difficulties facing the American people in the post-Revolu-
tionary period. "I think he will. . . ."[23] And to David Humphreys he wrote on March 23, 1793:

If it can be esteemed a happiness to live in an age productive of
great and interesting events, we of the present age are highly
favoured. The rapidity of national revolutions appear[s] no less
astonishing than their magnitude. In what they will terminate, is
known only to the great ruler of events; and confiding in his
wisdom and goodness, we may safely trust the issue to him, without perplexing ourselves to seek for that, which is beyond human
ken; only taking care to perform the parts assigned us, in a way
that reason and our own conscience approve of.[24]

For Washington, then, obviously, Providence was, in the
third place, a "benign" and "beneficient Being."[25] It was,
as he variously called it, the "Supreme Author of all Good,"[26]
a "Gracious and all kind Providence,"[27] the "Supreme Dispenser of every Good,"[28] the "author of all care and good."[29]
Its ultimate goal, he once said, was "to bring round the
greatest degree of happiness to the greatest number of his
people."[30] "Providence," he told his brother Lund, "to whom
we are infinitely more indebted than we are to our own
wisdom, or our own exertions, has always displayed its power
and goodness, when clouds and thick darkness seemed ready
to overwhelm us."[31]

At critical junctures during the American Revolution and while he was President, Washington felt that he could always be sure of the "Smiles of a kind Providence" on the American cause.[32] "How it will end," he told Joseph Reed early in 1776, "God in his great goodness will direct. I am thankful for his protection to this time."[33] "We have nothing my Dear Sir, to depend upon," he wrote John Adams a few months later, "but the protection of a kind Providence and unanimity among ourselves."[34] And Washington believed that his faith in "the blessings of a benign Providence" was always fully justified by subsequent events.[35] A "bountiful Providence," he told his brother John Augustine Washington in 1778, "has never failed us in the hour of distress."[36] He was always able to count on "the great Ruler of events," he told Samuel Bishop, mayor of New Haven, in 1793, for "his preserving goodness."[37]

Washington relied on the justice, as well as on the power, wisdom, and goodness, of Providence. Its decrees, he told Bryan Fairfax, were "always just and wise."[38] People who respected "the eternal rules of order and right, which Heaven itself has ordained," he insisted, could look forward with confidence to "the propitious smiles of Heaven" on their endeavors.[39] "I will not lament or repine at any acts of Providence," he wrote Joseph Reed in 1776, "because I am in a great measure a convert to Mr. Pope's opinion that whatever is, is right. . . ."[40] In fighting for their own independence from Great Britain, the American people, Washington felt, were also championing the cause of universal justice, and thus there was "every reason to expect Heaven will crown with Success, so just a cause."[41] For victory in the Revolution, Washington declared at the end of the war, "the praise is due to the *Grand Architect* of the Universe; who did not see fit to suffer his Superstructures and justice to be subjected to the ambition of the princes of the World, or to the rod of oppression, in the hands of any power upon Earth."[42]

And yet, having affirmed all of this, Washington acknowledged that there always remained something indefinably elusive about Providence. The "ways of Providence" were, he confessed, ultimately "inscrutable."[43] Not all of its "wise purposes" were "discoverable by finite minds."[44] There were many "acts of Providence" which "no human foresight" could "guard against."[45] The "great governor of the Universe," he said, frequently "causes contingencies" which baffle even the wisest of men.[46]

Still, the "invisible workings of Providence" were often the occasion for deep gratitude as well as genuine astonishment.[47] Washington could never look back upon the victory of the American people, against great odds, in the Revolutionary War, or their success in establishing orderly and stable government under the federal Constitution, without being impressed with the "invisible hand" which seemed to be shaping the destiny of the new nation.[48] As he told William Tudor shortly before the inauguration of the new federal government,

A multiplication of circumstances, scarcely yet investigated, appears to have co-operated in bringing about the great, and I trust happy, revolution, that is on the eve of being accomplished. It will not be uncommon that those things, which were considered at the moment as real ills, should have been no inconsiderable causes in producing positive and permanent national felicity. For it is thus that Providence works in the mysterious course of events "from seeming evil still educing good."[49]

A few days later he expressed the same thought to Annis

Boudinot Stockton: "I can never trace the concatenation of causes which led to these events, without acknowledging the mystery and admiring the goodness of Providence. To that superintending Power alone is our retraction from the brink of ruin to be attributed."[50]

On the other hand, when he reflected on the bloody upheaval in Europe following the French Revolution (from which, at first, he had expected so much good to follow), he confessed himself to be utterly perplexed by the mysterious "designs of Providence."[51] In a letter to the Earl of Buchan from Philadelphia on May 26, 1794, he expressed a heartfelt wish that human beings would devote their efforts to philanthropy, industry, manufacturing, and the arts, rather than to war and bloodshed. "But," he added,

providence, for purposes beyond the reach of mortal scan, has suffered the restless and malignant passions of man, the ambitions and sordid views of those who direct them, to keep the affairs of this world in a continual state of disquietude; and will, it is to be feared, place the prospects of peace too far off, and the promised millenium at an awful distance from our day.[52]

And, discussing the critical relations between the United States and France in 1798 with President John Adams, he cried out: "But this seems to be the Age of Wonders! and reserved for intoxicated and lawless France (for purposes of Providence far beyond the reach of human ken) to slaughter its own Citizens, and to disturb the repose of all the world besides."[53] The ways of Providence, he told Thaddeus Kosciuszko, were indeed inscrutable; and "Mortals must submit."[54] Many years before this he had tried to console Burwell Bassett for the death of his daughter by pointing out that the ways of Providence being inscrutable, and the justice of it not to be scanned by the shallow eye of humanity, not to be counteracted by the utmost efforts of human power or wisdom, resignation, and as far as the strength of our reason and religion can carry us, a cheerful acquiescence to the Divine Will, is what we are to aim. . . .[55]

The marked strain of determinism that ran through Washington's religious thought was not, it is apparent from his own career, accompanied by resignation, submission, or quietism as regards the things of this world. Quite the contrary. His faith in what he called providential determinations filled his life with an unshakable sense of direction and purposefulness that prevented him from abandoning the struggle to go forward even when the future seemed most dark and unpromising. No matter what the odds, the human struggle was always worthwhile for Washington. Like the old-fashioned predestinarian Calvinist (and like many modern secular determinists), Washington was stimulated and energized psychologically by the conviction that the course of events followed an orderly pattern and was not the product of mere blind, senseless chance. Nothing, after all, in his philosophy, was pointless. The moral struggle was never futile. What he did and what other human beings did, as well as what happened in the universe at large that was beyond man's control, were always of significance. No matter how great the obstacles or heartbreaking the perplexities that confronted him as Continental Commander and as President, his belief that a wise and just Providence was at work in the world enabled him to put forth his best efforts. That the purposes of Providence were ultimately unfathomable by human minds filled him with humility and a consciousness of his own shortcomings and protected him against

arrogance in victory. But that a wise and beneficent Providence was certain to favor the cause of justice and righteousness, as Washington conceived them, filled him with courage
and resolution and protected him against despair in failure.
As a man of action, Washington combined equanimity with
determination. "I look upon every dispensation of Providence
as designed to answer some valuable purpose," he wrote
Lund Washington in May, 1779, "and I hope I shall always
possess a sufficient degree of fortitude to bear without mur-
muring any stroke which may happen, either to my person,
or estate, from that quarter." "But," he added with feeling,

I cannot, with any degree of patience, behold the infamous practices of speculators, monopolizers, and all that class of gentry
which are preying upon our very vitals, and, for the sake of a
little dirty pelf, are putting the rights and liberties of the country
into the most imminent danger. . . .[56]

The implication was clear enough: the American people
could expect the "smiles of Providence" upon their endeavors
only if they exerted themselves to the utmost in matters
which it was in their power to control.

This theme—God helps those who help themselves—has
a quaint ring today, but it was a favorite of Washington's.
Washington invariably linked "the smiles of Providence"
with "Vigorous Exertions" on the part of the American
people.[57] This was especially true during the Revolution. "If
we make Freedom our choice," he declared in August, 1776,
"we must obtain it, by the Blessing of Heaven on our United
and Vigorous Efforts."[58] It would be folly, he told Brigadier
General Samuel Holden Parsons in April, 1777, to expect that
Providence "who has already done much for us, would
continue his gracious interposition and work miracles for

our deliverance, without troubling ourselves about the matter."[59]

In a letter to Brigadier General Thomas Nelson in which
he expressed disappointment over the outcome of the Battle
of Germantown in November, 1777, he said firmly: "We
must endeavour to deserve better of Providence, and, I am
persuaded, she will smile on us."[60] On March 18, 1779, he
wrote John Armstrong, delegate to the Continental Congress
from Pennsylvania, to say:

The hour . . . is certainly come when party differences and disputes should subside; when every Man (especially those in Office)
should with one hand and one heart pull the same way and with
their whole strength. Providence has done, and I am persuaded
is disposed to do, a great deal for us, but we are not to forget
the fable of Jupiter and the Countrymen.[61]

The end of the war did not mean that there could be
any relaxation of efforts by the American people. They must
continue to work hard at the tasks of postwar reconstruction
if they were to deserve the continuing favor of Providence.
"Providence has done much for us," he told James McHenry,
Maryland delegate in Congress, shortly after the conclusion
of a preliminary peace with Britain, "but we must do something for ourselves, if we expect to go triumphantly through
with it."[62] In notes which he jotted down for one of his
addresses shortly after he became President, Washington
planned to tell the first Congress: "Such exertions of your
talents will render your situations truly dignified and cannot
fail of being acceptable in the sight of the Divinity."[63] In
a letter to John Jay on the eve of Jay's mission to England
in 1794, Washington pointed out that

it is hardly possible in the early stages of a negociation to foresee all the results, so much depending on fortuitous circumstances, and incidents which are not within our controul; so, to deserve success, by employing the means with which we are possessed, to the best advantage, and trusting the rest to the all wise disposer, is all that an enlightened public, and the virtuous and well disposed part of the community, can reasonably expect; nor in which will they I am sure be disappointed.[64]

In addition to acting with spirit and vigor, human beings must strive at all times to act intelligently and decently if they wished to have the "smiles of Providence" bestowed upon their endeavors. Providence, as we have seen, represented wisdom and justice, as well as beneficence, for Washington, and in his opinion it could be expected to support only wise and just courses of action. Of the justice of the Revolutionary cause Washington was, of course, utterly convinced. As he told John Augustine Washington in May, 1776, ". . . it is to be hoped, that if our cause is just, as I do most religiously believe it to be, the same Providence which has in many Instances appear'd for us, will still go on to afford it aid."[65] Since "Liberty, Honor, and Safety are all at stake," he declared in August, 1776, "Providence will smile upon our Efforts, and establish us once more, the Inhabitants of a free and happy country."[66] During the crisis with France in 1798, Washington also believed that justice was on the side of the American people and that American policy toward France merited the approval of Providence. To President Adams he wrote from Mount Vernon on July 13, 1798:

Satisfied therefore, that you have sincerely wished and endeavoured to avert war, and exhausted to the last drop, the cup of reconciliation, we can with pure hearts appeal to Heaven for the justice of our cause, and may confidently trust the final result to that kind Providence who has heretofore, and so often, signally favoured the People of these United States.[67]

He expressed the same idea to Rev. Jonathan Boucher the following month:

What will be the consequence of our Arming for self defence, that Providence, who permits these doings in the Disturbers of Mankind; and who rules and Governs all things, alone can tell. To its all powerful decrees we must submit, whilst we hope that the justice of our Cause, if War, must ensue, will entitle us to its protection.[68]

On the other hand, Washington did not self-righteously identify everything the American people did with the will of God. He was frequently distressed by the behavior of his fellow-countrymen and more than once he warned that the American people could scarcely expect the divine favor if they acted foolishly or unjustly. Disturbed by the provincial jealousies and quarrels that reappeared at the close of the Revolutionary War and threatened to jeopardize the unity and security of the newly independent nation, Washington wrote Governor Jonathan Trumbull of Connecticut in 1784 that the "All Wise, and all powerful director of human events [may] suffer our indiscretions and folly to place our national character low in the political Scale; and this, unless more wisdom and less prejudice take the lead in our governments, will most assuredly be the case."[69] In notes for an address to Congress which he prepared in April, 1789, but which he never used, Washington planned to make the same point: "If the blessings of Heaven showered thick around us should be spilled on the ground or converted to curses, through the fault of those for whom they were intended, it would not be the first instance of folly or perverseness in short-sighted mortals."[70] By September, however, he was more hopeful. "The man must be bad indeed," he told Rev. Samuel Langdon,

who can look upon the events of the American Revolution without feeling the warmest gratitude towards the great Author of the Universe whose divine interposition was so frequently manifested in our behalf. And it is my earnest prayer that we may so conduct ourselves as to merit a continuance of those blessings with which we have hitherto been favored.[71]

With that characteristic modesty that is possible only to persons with genuine strength of character and personality, Washington always responded, in private as well as in public, to the accolades of his countrymen for his leadership in war and in peace by insisting that he had only acted as an "instrument" of Providence.[72] "To the Great ruler of events," he told Jonathan Williams in March, 1795, "not to any exertions of mine, is to be ascribed the favourable termination of our late contest for liberty. I never considered the fortunate issue of any measure in any other light than as the ordering of a kind Providence. . . ."[73]

Washington remembered only too vividly the terrible difficulties he had faced during the Revolution in holding the Continental Army together and seeing that it was properly trained, fed, clothed, and equipped. He was genuinely astonished when he looked back on the events of the Revolution. The achievement of victory in the face of almost insuperable obstacles seemed to him little short of a miracle. That the "interpositions of Providence" had been a major factor in the outcome of the Revolution he had no doubt.[74]

"The hand of Providence has been so conspicuous in all this," he told Brigadier General Nelson, "that he must be worse than an infidel that lacks faith, and more than wicked, that has not gratitude enough to acknowledge his obligations. . . ."[75] The Revolutionary struggle convinced him that Providence had singled out the American people for special attention and that if they made the most of "those blessings which God and Nature seemed to have intended us," they could anticipate "scenes of National happiness, which have not heretofore been offered for the fruition of the most favoured Nations."[76]

The work of the Constitutional Convention of 1787, the ratification of the Constitution by the requisite number of states during 1788, and the launching of the new federal government in 1789 seemed to Washington ample justification for his belief that "peculiar scenes of felicity" were reserved for the United States. "Indeed," he remarked to Lafayette, "I do not believe, that Providence has done so much for nothing."[77] With the adoption of the Constitution, he assured Charles Cotesworth Pinckney, "I think we may rationally indulge the pleasing hope that the Union will now be established upon a durable basis, and that Providence seems still disposed to favor the members of it, with unequalled opportunities for political happiness."[78] "No one," he wrote Benjamin Lincoln,

can rejoice more than I do at every step the people of this great country take to preserve the Union, establish good order and government, and to render the Nation happy at home and respectable abroad. No Country upon Earth ever had it more in its power to attain those blessings than United America. Wondrously strange, then, and much to be regretted indeed would it be, were we to neglect the means, and to depart from the road which Providence has pointed to us, so plainly; I cannot believe it will ever come to pass. The great Governor of the Universe has led us too long and too far on the road to happiness and glory, to forsake us in the midst of it.[79]

"I am sure," he told John Armstrong in 1792,

there never was a people who had more reason to acknowledge a divine interposition in their affairs, than those of the United States; and I should be pained to believe that they have forgotten that agency, which was so often manifested during our Revolution, or that they failed to consider the omnipotence of that God who is alone able to protect them.[80]

And what of Washington himself? How did he relate his own life to the "interpositions" of Providence which he saw so conspicuously at work in the affairs of his country?[81] In a letter to his wife in June, 1775, following his appointment as Commander in Chief of the Continental Army, Washington described the "inexpressible concern" which he felt over the momentous responsibility which he had just shouldered. Then he declared: "I shall rely, therefore, confidently on that Providence, which has heretofore preserved and been bountiful to me, not doubting but that I shall return safe to you. . . ."[82]

Washington never had any personal doubts about the beneficence of Providence. His faith was eminently serene and untroubled. "Providence," he told Landon Carter, "has a . . . claim to my humble and grateful thanks, for its protection and direction of me."[83] He believed that the "finger of Providence" was tracing an orderly pattern in his own life as well as in the universe at large.[84] For Washington there were never any gnawing doubts about the existence of God; nor did he ever question the evidences of providential design in creation. Belonging essentially to that class of psychologically (and hence philosophically) untroubled temperaments which William James called the "once-born," he never agonized about his deepest convictions. The problem of evil left him undisturbed. Whatever shortcomings he recognized in man, he never doubted the ultimate wisdom and goodness of the decrees of the Almighty.

At the same time, there was something unmistakably remote and abstract (even, at times, tautological) about the Providence on which Washington relied so confidently throughout his life. He rarely spoke of Providence in personal terms. He did, it is true, assure his friends before assuming the presidency that "the great Searcher of human hearts is my witness, that I have no wish, which aspires beyond the humble and happy lot of living and dying a private citizen on my own farm."[85] But the allusion to "Searcher of human hearts" here was unusual for him. In the main, Washington's God was an impersonal force with whose decrees the efforts of human beings (whose freedom to choose was presumably part of the providential plan) somehow always balanced out in the end. It cannot be said that Washington ever experienced any feeling of personal intimacy or communion with his God; nor does the aesthetic side of religion—the poetic beauty of scriptural passages or the liturgy of the Anglican church—seem to have had any great appeal for him. His allusions to religion are almost totally lacking in depths of feeling. Writing to Major General Henry Knox at the end of the Revolution, he declared,

I feel now . . . as I conceive a wearied Traveller must do, who, after treading many a painful step, with a heavy burden on his shoulders, is eased of the latter, having reached the Goal to which all the former were directed; and from his House top is looking back, and tracing with a grateful eye the Meanders by which he escaped the quicksands and Mires which lay in his way; and into which none but the All-powerful guide, and great disposer of human Events could have prevented his falling.[86]

And to Rev. William Gordon he remarked toward the end of his life that he was "grateful to that Providence which has directed my steps, and shielded me in the various changes and chances, through which I have passed, from my youth to the present moment."[87] Though eminently a man of action, not of reflection, Washington had a faith that was essentially of the mind, not of the heart. Rarely did it engage the emotional side of his nature. If he was untroubled by doubts and anxieties, he was also untouched by the alternating states of exaltation and despair that possessed such a passionately committed believer as his contemporary Benjamin Rush.

Washington faced death, as he had faced life, with complete equanimity. It was an integral part of the divine order of things and was to be met with resignation and fortitude. In reconciling oneself to death, Washington invariably reminded his bereaved friends, one could take comfort in and derive consolation from the knowledge that the passing of loved ones fitted somehow into the wise and just, though ultimately mysterious, purposes of a beneficent Providence. They were "acts of Providence, and in themselves unavoidable"; hence, "acquiescence to the divine will is not only a duty, but is to be aided by every manly exertion to forget the causes of such uneasiness."[88] By submitting patiently to "the decrees of the Allwise disposer of Human events," one could "find the only true and substantial comfort under the greatest of calamities."[89] The "will of Heaven," he told George

Augustine Washington in January, 1793, "is not to be con-
troverted or scrutinized by the children of this world. It
therefore becomes the Creatures of it to submit with patience
and resignation to the will of the Creator whether it be to
prolong, or to shorten the number of days."[90]

"He that gave you know has a right to take away," he
consoled his Secretary of War, Henry Knox, in 1791, on the
death of Knox's son; "his ways are wise, they are inscrutable,
and irresistible."[91] Regarding the death of his own nephew in
1793, Washington told Bryan Fairfax: "It is a loss I sincerely
regret, but as it is the will of Heaven, whose decrees are
always just and wise, I submit to it without a murmur."[92]
The "Dispensations of Providence are as inscrutable, as they
are wise and uncontroulable," he said when he heard of the
death of Tobias Lear's wife. "It is the duty therefore of
Religion and Philosophy, to submit to its decrees, with as
little repining as the sensibility of our natures, will permit."[93]
Regarding the passing of Patrick Henry, only a few months
before his own death, Washington told Archibald Blair:

At any time I should have recd. the account of this Gentleman's
death with sorrow. In the present crisis of our public affairs, I
have heard it with deep regret. But the ways of Providence are
inscrutable, and not to be scanned by short sighted man; whose
duty is submission, without repining at its decrees.[94]

When it came to "looking into doomsday book" himself,
as he once put it, Washington's attitude was one of cheerful
acquiescence as well as imperturbable calm.[95] In a whimsical
letter which he composed for his wife to send to Mrs. Elizabeth Powel in December, 1797, appears this passage:

I am now, by desire of the General, to add a few words on his behalf, which he desired may be expressed in the terms following, that is, to say—that disparing of hearing what may be said of him, if he should really go off in an apopleptic fit or any other fit (for he thinks all fits that issue in death are worse than a love fit or a fit of laughter, and many other kinds which he could name) he is glad to hear before hand what will be said of him on that occasion; conceiving that nothing extra will happen between this and then, to make a change in his character—for better or for worse—and besides he had entered into an engagement with Mr. Morris and several other Gentlemen not to quitt the theatre of this world before the year 1800, it may be relied upon that no breach of contract shall be laid to him on that account unless dire necessity should bring about maugre all his exertions to the contrary. In that case, he shall hope they would do by him as he would do by them, excuse it; at present there seems to be no danger of his giving them the slip, as neither his health nor his spirits were ever in greater glow, notwithstanding, he adds, he is descending and has almost reached the bottom of the hill, or in other words, the shades below.[96]

Three months before his death, speaking of the recent passing of his brother Samuel, Washington told Colonel Burgess Ball: "I was the *first,* and am now the *last* of my fathers Children by the second marriage who remain. When I shall be called upon to follow them, is known only to the giver of life. When the summons comes I shall endeavour to obey it with a good grace."[97]

There is some evidence, though it is far from conclusive, that Washington believed in immortality. When one of his associates named a son after him, Washington wrote to express the hope that "he will live long to enjoy it, long after I have taken my departure for the world of Spirits."[98] In a letter to Jonathan Trumbull, Jr., at the close of the Revolution, Washington asked his former military secretary to assure his father, the governor of Connecticut, that it is my wish, the mutual friendship and esteem which have been planted and fostered in the tumult of public life, may not wither and die in the serenity of retirement: tell him we should rather amuse our evening hours of Life in cultivating the tender plants, and bringing them to perfection, before they are translated to a happier clime.[99]

Writing to Annis Boudinot Stockton in 1788, Washington remarked in passing: ". . . with Cicero in speaking respecting his belief of the immortality of the Soul, I will say, if I am in a grateful delusion, it is an innocent one, and I am willing to remain under its influence."[100]

When his mother died in August, 1789, at the age of eighty-three, he wrote his sister, Elizabeth Washington Lewis, to express the hope that "she is translated to a happier place."[101] Speaking of the affairs of his estate in a letter to Secretary of War James McHenry a few months before his death, Washington explained: "My greatest anxiety is to leave all these concerns in such a clear, and distinct form, as that no reproach may attach itself to me, when I have taken my departure for the land of Spirits."[102]

How literally these scattered references to a "happier clime" and a "land of Spirits" may be taken it is not possible to say. Certainly there is an aloof and impersonal tone about all of them just as, indeed, there was about what Washington once called his "Doctrine of Providence." Thomas Paine, by contrast, announced frankly in *The Age of Reason* that "I hope for happiness beyond this life"; Benjamin Franklin affirmed to Ezra Stiles his belief that "the soul of Man is immortal, and will be treated with Justice in another Life respecting its Conduct in this";[103] and Thomas Jefferson expected upon death "to ascend in essence to an ecstatic meeting with the friends we have loved and lost, and whom we shall still love and never lose again."[104] If Washington did in fact share the hopes of these contemporaries, which seems likely, he never got around to saying so except in the vaguest fashion.

In his last hours, Washington acted as he had hoped to—"with a good grace." "Doctor, I die hard, but I am not afraid to go," he told one of the physicians at his bedside.[105] According to Parson Weems, when the end came Washington folded his arms "decently on his breast, then breathing out *'Father of mercies, take me to thyself,'*—he fell asleep."[106] In fact, Washington said nothing of the kind in his last moments. Tobias Lear, his secretary, who was with him to the end, has described the final scene:

> About ten o'clk he made several attempts to speak to me before he could effect it, at length he said,—*"I am just going. Have me decently buried; and do not let my body be put into the vault in less than three days after I am dead."* I bowed assent, for I could not speak. He then looked at me again and said, *"Do you understand me?"* I replied, "Yes." " 'Tis well," said he.
>
> About ten minutes before he expired (which was between ten & eleven o'clk) his breathing became easier; he lay quietly;—he withdrew his hand from mine, and felt his own pulse. I saw his countenance change. I spoke to Dr. Craik who sat by the fire;—he came to the bed side. The General's hand fell from his wrist—I took it in mine and put it into my bosom. Dr. Craik put his hands over his eyes and he expired without a struggle or a sigh![107]

Thus Washington died, as he had lived, with simplicity and dignity. That he neglected to call for a clergyman and failed to utter words of a religious nature at the very end has been a source of great disappointment to the pietists. There is no question, however, that "Reason, religion, and philosophy"—which he was fond of urging on his friends as sources for consolation in times of sorrow—had long since reconciled him to his departure from this life.[108]

Moncure D. Conway, a liberal Protestant writing in the late nineteenth century, found something "hard and mechanical" in Washington's religious outlook. "It does not impress me as a true or happy or beautiful faith . . . ," he declared. "I feel about Washington . . . that his character might have been more sympathetic and his life happier, had he felt some of the enthusiasm of humanity now represented by Jesus in the Broad Church."[109] Whether Washington's life would have been happier and his character more sympathetic had he shared Conway's own liberal Protestant views is, of course, a matter of opinion. It is also open to question whether Washington would have lived a more fruitful life had he pondered more deeply and systematically on the nature of things as his friends Benjamin Franklin, John Adams, and Thomas Jefferson did. Washington was, after all, primarily a doer rather than a thinker. His religious principles, as he confessed, were "few and simple." Whatever their shortcomings—and surely they have little to say to thoughtful twentieth-century Americans who have to find their way amid the ruins of the universal moral and intellectual order whose objective existence Washington and his fellow-Deists took for granted—they did enable him to live his life with honor and integrity. He always tried to walk "on a straight line," he once told Bryan Fairfax, "and endeavoured as far as human frailties, and perhaps strong passions, would enable him, to discharge the relative duties to his Maker and fellow-men, without seeking any indirect or left handed attempts to acquire popularity."[110] There was a rugged honesty in Washington's stubborn refusal to "acquire popularity" by assuming religious postures in public that he did not feel privately.

Washington's religious principles were ways in which he accommodated himself personally to the inescapable recalcitrancies and implacable mysteries of human existence. He did not, as a public figure, pretend to speak for the American people in matters of religion. His preference was for a pluralistic society in which Protestant, Catholic, Jew, Deist, and freethinker were free to come to terms with the universe in their own fashion; and it was this conception of America, not any particular religious views of his own, that he sought to encourage in public statements during his presidency. "With the sublime taciturnity which had marked his life," Moncure Conway acknowledged, "he passed out of existence, leaving no act or word which can be turned to the service of superstition, cant, or bigotry."[111] Washington's refusal to do or say anything that would serve the cause of superstition and bigotry set a noble example for the American people. It was one of his greatest contributions to the American heritage and it deserves serious examination.

VI

WASHINGTON
AND RELIGIOUS LIBERTY

DURING THE COURSE of a speech delivered in October, 1958, on the occasion of the laying of the cornerstone of the Inter-Church Center in New York City, President Eisenhower declared:

We are politically free people because each of us is free to express his individual faith. As Washington said in 1793, so we can say today: "We have abundant reason to rejoice that in this land the light of truth and reason has triumphed over the power of bigotry and superstition, and that every person may here worship God according to the dictates of his own heart."

Then, expressing his "horror" at the recent bombing of a Jewish synagogue in Atlanta, Georgia, he added: "You can imagine the outrage that would have been expressed by our first President today had he read in the news dispatches of the bombing of a synagogue."[1]

Washington would indeed have been outraged. More than once, in private letters and in public statements, the

116

first President voiced his utter detestation of intolerance, prejudice, and "every species of religious persecution."[2] His often-expressed wish was, as he told the New Church Society (Swedenborgian) in Baltimore in an address from which President Eisenhower quoted, that "bigotry and superstition" would be overcome by "truth and reason" in the United States (Appendix, 27). And in the fight against bigotry Washington himself played a role second to none. Both as Commander in Chief of the Continental Army and as President of the United States, he always used his immense prestige and influence to encourage mutual tolerance and good will among American Protestants, Catholics, and Jews, and to create a climate of opinion in which every citizen (as he told the Jewish community in Newport, Rhode Island) "shall sit in safety under his own vine and fig tree and there shall be none to make him afraid" (Appendix, 21).

The fact is that Washington was no less firmly committed to religious liberty and freedom of conscience than were Thomas Jefferson and James Madison. Like Jefferson and Madison, he looked upon the new nation over whose fortunes he presided as a pluralistic society in which people with varied religious persuasions and nationality backgrounds learned to live peacefully and rationally together instead of resorting to force and violence. In his opinion, what was unique about the United States, in fact, in addition to "cheapness of land," was the existence of "civil and religious liberty" which "stand perhaps unrivalled by any civilized nation of earth."[3] In his General Orders for April 18, 1783, announcing the cessation of hostilities with Great Britain, he congratulated his soldiers, "of whatever condition they may be," for, among other things, having "assisted in protecting the rights of human nature and establishing an Asylum for the poor and oppressed of all nations and religions. . . ."⁴ The "bosom of America," he declared a few months later, was "open to receive . . . the oppressed and persecuted of all Nations and Religions; whom we shall welcome to a participation of all our rights and privileges."⁵ The following year, when asking Tench Tilghman to secure a carpenter and a bricklayer for his Mount Vernon estate, he remarked: "If they are good workmen, they may be of Asia, Africa, or Europe. They may be Mohometans, Jews or Christians of any Sect, or they may be Atheists."⁶ As he told a Mennonite minister who sought refuge in the United States after the Revolution: "I had always hoped that this land might become a safe and agreeable Asylum to the virtuous and persecuted part of mankind, to whatever nation they might belong. . . ."⁷ He was, as John Bell pointed out in 1779, "a total stranger to religious prejudices, which have so often excited Christians of one denomination to cut the throats of those of another."⁸

It is difficult, if not impossible, to determine exactly when and by what process Washington became "a total stranger to religious prejudices." In Virginia, the Anglican church to which he belonged was established by law before the Revolution and occupied a preferential position in Virginia society. The Virginia establishment had become considerably liberalized during the eighteenth century; nevertheless, dissenting groups, like the Baptists, were subjected to a variety of legal disabilities and on occasion experienced a good deal of open persecution. Baptist historians, indeed, sometimes explain Washington's deep-seated devotion to the principle of religious freedom as growing out of his revulsion against the wave of mobbings and jailings of Baptists that took place in Virginia on the eve of the Revolution.[9] This, we know, played some part in the development of Madison's views on religious liberty; but as for Washington, there is no evidence available that he was ever cognizant of these events.[10]

There is evidence, however, that Washington learned very early the economic disadvantages that frequently accompany legal restrictions on religion. When he was about eighteen, his elder half-brother, Lawrence, became deeply involved, as a member of the Ohio Company, in negotiations for the sale of fifty thousand acres of land beyond the Alleghenies to a group of Pennsylvania Germans. The Germans wanted to purchase the land, but, as dissenters, they were unwilling to pay taxes to support the Anglican church; and Lawrence was attempting to persuade the Virginia Assembly to pass an act exempting them from the parish levies. "I am well assured," he wrote in discouragement to John Hanbury, the Ohio Company's English partner, in April, 1751, "we shall never obtain it by a law here." He went on to say:

It has been my opinion, and I hope ever will be, that restraints on conscience are cruel, in regard to those on whom they are imposed, and injurious to the country imposing them. England, Holland, and Prussia I may quote as examples, and much more Pennsylvania, which has flourished under that delightful liberty, so as to become the admiration of every man, who considers the short time it has been settled. . . . This Colony [Virginia] was greatly settled in the latter part of Charles the First's time, and during the usurpation, by the zealous churchmen; and that spirit, which was then brought in, has ever since continued, so that except a few Quakers we have no dissenters. But what has been the consequence? We have increased by slow degrees . . . , whilst our neighbouring colonies, whose natural advantages are greatly inferior to ours, have become populous.[11]

The conviction that restraints on conscience are both "cruel" to the victims and "injurious" to those imposing them, George may well have learned from his brother. Biographers are generally agreed that Lawrence was a major influence on the young Washington. Many years later, when George himself was attempting to import some Germans from the Palatinate to settle on his western lands, he emphasized the fact that he saw "no prospect of these people being restrained in the smallest degree, either in their civil or religious principles; which I take notice of, because these are privileges, which mankind are solicitous to enjoy, and emigrants must be anxious to know."[12] Like his brother, Washington seems to have been aware of the principle involved as well as the expediency of extending religious liberty to prospective settlers.

Washington's personal views in the broader realm of religious faith are also undoubtedly relevant to an understanding of his attitude toward religious liberty. He was, as we have seen, completely lacking in creedal commitment of any kind; and his infrequent references, in public and in private, to the Christian religion were of an exceedingly formal nature. At times, in fact, Washington wrote as if he considered himself an outsider. In a letter to Lafayette in 1787 in which he commented hopefully on the Frenchman's "plan of toleration in religious matters" for France, he explained: "Being no bigot myself to any mode of worship, I am disposed to indulge the professors of Christianity in the church, that road to Heaven which to them shall seem the most direct plainest easiest and least liable to exception."[13] This sense of detachment, tinged with irony, appears even more clearly in a letter to Sir Edward Newenham in 1792 when he was discussing the controversies between Protestants and Catholics in Ireland:

Of all the animosities which have existed among mankind, those which are caused by a difference of sentiments in religion appear to me the most inveterate and distressing, and ought most to be deprecated. I was in hopes, that the enlightened and liberal policy, which has marked the present age, would at least have reconciled *Christians* of every denomination so far, that we should never again see their religious disputes carried to such a pitch as to endanger the peace of Society.[14]

It is clear that Washington's devotion to religious liberty was not based, like Roger Williams', upon a profound and passionate conviction that freedom was crucial for the Christian earthly pilgrimage. Washington seems to have had the characteristic unconcern of the eighteenth-century Deist for the forms and creeds of institutional religion. He had, moreover, the strong aversion of the upper-class Deist for sectarian quarrels that threatened to upset the "peace of Society." It is a truism that indifference leads to toleration, and no doubt Washington's Deist indifference to sectarian concerns was an important factor in producing the broad-minded tolerance in matters of religion which he displayed throughout his life.

Still, like most American Deists (and unlike many European Deists), Washington, as we have seen, had little or none of the anticlerical spirit. In addition to attending his own church with a fair degree of regularity, he also visited other churches, including the Roman Catholic, on occasion. Moreover, from time to time, like Franklin and Jefferson, he contributed money to the building funds of denominations other than his own. And he had no objection, at first, to the proposal of the Virginia legislature to levy a general tax for the support of the churches of the state following the dis-establishment of the Anglican church after the Revolution. "Altho. no man's sentiments are more opposed to *any kind* of restraint upon religious principles than mine are," he told George Mason,

yet I must confess, that I am not amongst the number of those who are so much alarmed at the thoughts of making people pay towards the support of that which they profess, if of the denomi-nation of Christians; or declare themselves Jews, Mahomitans or otherwise, and thereby obtain proper relief.

Having learned, however, of the "disquiet of a respectable minority" over the assessment plan and fearing that its adop-tion would "rankle and perhaps convulse, the State," he expressed his regret that the issue had been raised and hoped that "the Bill could die an easy death."[15] The agitation over the Virginia assessment plan seems to have convinced him, once and for all, of the impracticality of all proposals of this kind for state support of religion.

But it would be wrong to assume that Washington's views were shaped solely by social expediency and theological indifference. Though Washington was not given much to philosophical reflection, he did, on one occasion at least, try to work out a more fundamental basis for his views on lib-erty. In a fragmentary passage in his handwriting that he apparently intended to use in his Inaugural Address or in his first annual message to Congress, Washington asked:

[Should I] set up my judgment as the standard of perfection?

And shall I arrogantly pronounce that whosoever differs from me, must discern the subject through a distorting medium, or be influenced by some nefarious scheme? The mind is so formed in different persons as to contemplate the same objects in different points of view. Hence originates the difference on questions of the greatest import, human and divine.[16]

Without reading too much into this isolated passage, it may be noted that Washington's apparent attempt here to find a basis for liberty in a pluralistic view of human perceptions sounds very much like Jefferson. Differences of opinion, Jefferson always insisted, "like differences of face, are a law of our own nature, and should be viewed with the same tolerance." Furthermore, such differences lead to inquiry and "inquiry to truth."[17] Freedom, therefore, for Jefferson, was a necessary condition for the moral and intellectual progress of mankind. Washington's musings on the eve of his inauguration are so Jeffersonian in spirit that one cannot help wondering whether his association with Jefferson had something to do with the clear-cut enunciation of his views on religious liberty that he made while he was President. At any rate, it was unquestionably a matter of principle with Washington to treat the "different points of view" of the religious organizations of his day on "questions of the greatest import" with sincere respect, even if he could not share these points of view. As he told Joseph Hopkinson toward the end of his life: "To expect that all men should think alike upon political, more than on Religious, or other subjects, would be to look for a change in the order of nature. . . ."[18] And since, as he said elsewhere, important questions are invariably "viewed through different mediums by different men, all that can be expected in such cases is charity [and] mutual forbearance. . . ."[19] Charity and mutual forbearance in matters of religion were for Washington prime desiderata in the life of the new nation.

During the Revolution Washington had little occasion to make formal pronouncements on the subject of religious freedom. Nevertheless, he made it clear, as Commander in Chief of the Continental Army, that he was firmly opposed to all expressions of religious bigotry among his soldiers. Roman Catholic historians frequently single out the fourteenth item of his instructions to Colonel Benedict Arnold on the eve of the Canadian expedition in the fall of 1775 to show that the American commander was "one of the very few men of the Revolution who had, in 1775, outgrown or overcome all religious prejudices in religious matters."[20] Washington's instructions on September 14 were these:

As the Contempt of the Religion of a Country by ridiculing any of its Ceremonies or affronting its Ministers or Votaries has ever been deeply resented, you are to be particularly careful to restrain every Officer and Soldier from such Imprudence and Folly and to punish every Instance of it. On the other hand, as far as lays in your power, you are to protect and support the free Exercise of the Religion of the Country and the undisturbed Enjoyment of the rights of Conscience in religious Matters, with your utmost Influence and Authority.[21]

In an accompanying letter to Arnold, Washington added:

I also give it in Charge to you to avoid all Disrespect to or Contempt of the Religion of the Country and its Ceremonies. Prudence, Policy, and a true Christian spirit, will lead us to look with Compassion upon their Errors without insulting them. While we are contending for our own Liberty, we should be very cautious of violating the Rights of Conscience in others, ever considering that God alone is the Judge of the Hearts of Men, and to him only in this Case, they are answerable.[22]

Obviously, "Prudence" and "Policy"—the hope of winning Canadian Catholics to the American cause—shaped Washington's orders as much as the "Rights of Conscience in others." Even the Continental Congress, which had made strongly anti-Catholic public statements regarding the Quebec Act in 1774, had learned to be solicitous of the welfare of Canadian Catholics by the fall of 1775. Moreover, the note of condescension in Washington's reference to Catholic "Errors" is unmistakable. Still, there is no evidence that Washington ever shared in the deep-seated anti-Catholic prejudice that existed in the colonies (Catholics were legally restricted in most of the thirteen colonies) on the eve of the Revolution. And although he criticized the Quebec Act, at no time did he ever join Hamilton and other patriot leaders in and outside of Congress in charging that its purpose was to establish "Popery" in the colonies. If his orders were not exactly "a model of the statesmanlike tolerance in religious matters which set Washington apart from so many of his contemporaries,"[23] they probably do show that he was "impatient of religious intolerance."[24]

A similar combination of policy and principle led Washington on November 5, 1775, to issue strict orders forbidding the celebration of "Pope's Day" (the colonial equivalent of Guy Fawkes' Day in England and especially popular in New England) among the troops at Cambridge:

As the Commander in Chief has been apprized of a design form'd for the observance of that ridiculous and childish custom of burning the Effigy of the pope—He cannot help expressing his surprise that there should be Officers and Soldiers in this army so void of common sense, as not to see the impropriety of such a step at this Juncture; at a Time when we are solliciting . . . the friendship and alliance of the people of Canada, whom we ought to consider as Brethren embarked in the same Cause. The defense of the general Liberty of America: at such a juncture and in such Circumstances, to be insulting their Religion, is so monstrous, as not to be suffered or excused. . . .[25]

While Washington's action on this occasion, as he made clear, was politically motivated, it is significant that his orders not only called attention to the "impropriety" of observing Pope's Day "at this Juncture," but also emphasized how "ridiculous and childish" the custom was. Catholic writers have generally looked upon his orders as those of "a brave and tolerant mind."[26] "Every Catholic heart in the colonies," declared Peter Guilday, "must have taken courage" at Washington's action.[27] "The insult to the Catholic religion," according to John Gilmary Shea, "was distasteful to his more liberal mind."[28] Martin Griffin called Washington "the destroyer of Pope's Day."[29] And, indeed, the observance of Pope's Day seems to have "received its death blow," as James Haltigan put it, "at the hands of the noble Washington."[30] There are no records of its celebration in America after 1775.[31] No doubt the decline in anti-Catholic feeling (resulting from the loyal support which American Catholics gave the Revolutionary cause and from the alliance with France) during the Revolutionary period accounts for the disappearance of the custom. Still, Washington was the first to put an end to anti-Catholic demonstrations of this kind, and the example he set undoubtedly carried great weight. By this action he won the profound gratitude of American Catholics.

During the Revolution Washington also endeared himself to American Universalists for upholding the right of John Murray, the founder of American Universalism, to officiate as chaplain in the Continental Army. The doctrine of universal salvation which Murray brought from England to the United States in 1770 had aroused bitter hostility among orthodox clergymen. By eliminating fear of hell, Murray's teaching, it was charged, undermined morality and led to atheism. Despite these charges, Murray won the admiration and friendship of influential laymen in New England before the Revolution; and in May, 1775, leading officers in the Rhode Island brigade, including Nathanael Greene and James Varnum, invited him to become their chaplain. Several weeks after Washington arrived in Cambridge to assume command of the troops around Boston, the rest of the chaplains united in presenting him with a petition asking for Murray's removal.[32] In his General Orders for September 17, however, Washington announced tersely: "The Revd. Mr. John Murray is appointed Chaplain to the Rhode-Island Regiments and is to be respected as such."[33] Like the Catholics, the Universalists have looked upon Washington as "noble-minded" and "immortal" for his insistence upon religious toleration in the Continental Army.[34] "History," said one writer of Washington's order regarding Chaplain Murray, "furnished no more signal instance of a rebuke of bigoted intolerance."[35] To a nineteenth-century historian of the Universalist church in the United States, Washington was an "immortal chief" with clear sympathies for the liberal doctrines of the Universalists.[36]

But Washington simply wanted his men to have, in so far as possible, chaplains of their own choosing. Moreover, he was eager to keep religious controversies out of the Continental Army. When Congress proposed, in 1777, substituting chaplains at the brigade level for the various regimental chaplains, Washington objected to the plan on the ground that it has a tendency to introduce religious disputes into the Army, which above all things should be avoided, and in many instances would compel men to a mode of Worship which they do not profess. The old Establishment gives every Regiment an Opportunity of having a Chaplain of their own religious Sentiments, it is founded on a plan of more generous toleration, and the choice of the Chaplains to officiate, has been generally in the Regiments. Supposing one Chaplain could do the duties of a Brigade, (which supposition However is inadmissable, when we view things in practice) that being composed of four or five, perhaps in some instances, Six Regiments, there might be so many different modes of Worship. I have mentioned the Opinion of the Officers and these hints to Congress upon this Subject; from a principle of duty and because I am well assured, it is most foreign to their wishes or intention to excite by any act, the smallest uneasiness or jealousy among the Troops.[37]

Washington's desire to keep religious friction at a minimum in the army and his determination to follow a policy of "generous toleration" for his fighting men was obviously plain common sense. Washington needed every man he could get and he knew (and others gradually learned) that Catholics and Universalists could be as good soldiers as anyone else. But what about men whose religious principles led them to refuse to bear arms in the cause? What was Washington's attitude toward the pacifist Quakers?

Washington had had some experience with the Quakers during the French and Indian War when he was serving as commander of all Virginia forces, with responsibility for frontier defenses. In 1756, six Quakers were drafted into the militia and sent to Winchester to fight under Washington. The young commander was genuinely perplexed by his first confrontation with Quaker pacifism. The six Quakers, he quickly learned, would "neither bear arms, work, receive provisions or pay, or do anything that tends, in any respect, to self-defense."[38] When Governor Dinwiddie advised him to "confine them with a short allowance of bread and water, till you bring them to reason,"[39] Washington reported that he "could by no means bring the Quakers to any terms. They chose rather to be whipped to death than bear arms, or lend us any assistance whatever upon the fort, or anything of self-defense."[40] The governor then sent these instructions: "Use them with lenity, but as they are at their own expense, I would have them remain as long as the other Draughts."[41] In a final reference to the problem, Washington wrote that, in compliance with these orders, the Quakers "still remain here, and shall until the other drafts are discharged."[42]

Washington's treatment of the six Quakers during the French and Indian War is sometimes cited as evidence of his early respect for the rights of conscience.[43] Actually, we know too little about the episode to draw any such conclusion. In any event, if Washington is to be commended for his restraint in the matter, the governor of Virginia must share in the commendation. Neither of them showed any special animus against the Quakers in their exchanges on the subject. There is, however, evidence that Virginia Quakers thought well of the young colonel. In July, 1758, shortly before Washington's election to the House of Burgesses, a friend of Washington's wrote to say of another candidate: "His interest I think declines among the Quakers, where I imagine your's is pretty good."[44]

Washington's first Revolutionary encounter with the Quakers took place during the siege of Boston. New England Quakers, assisted by donations from Quakers in Pennsylvania and New Jersey, organized a relief expedition to help the poor and needy in Boston and sent a committee of four to seek Washington's permission to enter the besieged city. Washington "received us kindly," Moses Brown, one of the chief planners of the project, said afterward,

but declined permitting us to go into Boston, saying he had made it a rule not to let any go in, unless it was a woman separated from her Husband or the like; but however, Showed a readiness, to further the designed distribution by proposing to send for some of our Friends to come out upon the lines ... for a Conferance with them.[45]

The committee "concluded to adopt that method."[46] As Brown explained later, "as the Small Pox was in Town ... our not being allowed to go in seemed a small or no disappointment."[47] The Quakers asked Washington for permission to write letters to General Howe explaining their plan and to two Quakers in Boston, through whom they hoped to distribute the relief, "which he concented to and proposed our shewing what we wrote to General Nathanael Greene."[48] Greene was a disowned Rhode Island Quaker whom Washington liked to tease about his pacifist background. "Sometimes," it was said, "Washington, who really loved a jest, would slyly remind him of his Quaker origin." As Brown recalled it, Washington told the committee: "Go to General Greene; he is a Quaker, and knows more about it than I do."[49] The committee accordingly sought out Greene, wrote the letters with his assistance, and submitted them to Washington that evening. Washington approved the letters and sent the Quakers, under a flag of truce, on to the British lines, where they arranged with General Howe for distributing funds among the war-sufferers of Boston.[50]

Moses Brown developed a sincere admiration of Washington as a result of his conversation with him in December, 1775. In after years he referred to him as a "great" man and spoke particularly of "his simple, easy manner."[51] And Washington's cordial reception of Brown and his associates and his readiness to co-operate in their undertaking testifies to his friendliness toward the Quakers (perhaps because of General Greene) during the early months of the war and to at least some appreciation of their pacifist-humanitarian principles.

With the Pennsylvania Quakers, however, Washington's relations were far less friendly. When the war shifted to Pennsylvania in 1777, Washington began to share the popular feeling among patriots generally that Quaker neutralism toward the war was, in essence, pro-British Toryism. It is true that in his correspondence with the Pennsylvania Council of Safety in January, 1777, regarding recruitment of men for the defense of Philadelphia, he took for granted the exemption of the "conscientiously scrupulous" from the draft and seems to have regarded this as unexceptionable.[52] By May, 1777, however, he was identifying the Quakers with the "disaffected" generally, charging them with attempting to obstruct the operation of the militia laws, and urging that steps be taken to defeat their "evil intentions."[53] His distrust of the Quakers reached a climax during the British occupation of Philadelphia. On two occasions at this time, in giving orders for the impressment of supplies from the countryside, he instructed his officers to bear down especially upon the "unfriendly Quakers and others notoriously disaffected to the cause of American liberty."[54] When the Quakers outside Philadelphia sought permission to send food into the city to help the needy during the British occupation, Washington flatly denied the request and even refused to see the delegation.[55] Moreover, in March, 1778, he ordered his officers to prohibit Quakers outside Philadelphia from entering the city to attend a meeting of the Society of Friends. "This is an intercourse that we should by all means endeavour to interrupt," he declared, "as the plans settled at these meetings are of the most pernicious tendency."[56]

Still, on other occasions during the same critical period of the war, when Washington was faced with a "Quaker problem," he reacted with kindness and consideration. In the summer of 1777, for example, several Quakers in western Virginia were drafted into the militia and marched about two hundred miles, with muskets tied to their backs, to Washington's camp outside Philadelphia. "But on their coming to the camp," related one of the draftees, "and the state of their case being represented to General Washington, they were, by his order discharged, and liberty given them to return home."[57] Washington's action, of course, followed from his belief that the "conscientiously scrupulous" should not be forced into the service and it has understandably received high praise from Quaker historians.[58]

Washington's polite reception of six delegates from the Philadelphia Yearly Meeting a few days after the Battle of Germantown has also won much praise from Quaker writers. The purpose of the delegation was twofold: to protest the arrest by Pennsylvania authorities of a number of leading Philadelphia Quakers, charged with pro-British sympathies, and their exile to Winchester, Virginia; and to clear the Society of Friends of charges that it was transmitting intelligence to the British.[59] With them the delegates carried a

"Testimony against War," explaining why the Quakers "are led out of all wars & Fightings," denying any "Correspondence highly prejudicial to the public Safety," and requesting that the Virginia exiles be restored "to their afflicted Families & Friends."[60] The delegates first visited General Howe, who received them good-naturedly, and then proceeded to Washington's camp, where they "had a very full Opportunity of clearing the Society from the Aspersions which had been invidiously raised against them, and distributed a number of the Testimonies amongst the Officers, who received them and made no objections."[61]

Warner Mifflin, apparently the leader of the group, was said to have been greeted by Washington "with open arms" and "entertained and made much of by everyone around."[62] By everyone, perhaps, but General John Armstrong, who remarked waspishly the following day: "We lost a great part of yesterday with a deputation of Quakers from their yearly meeting."[63] The delegates later reported simply that "we were kindly entertained by General Washington,"[64] but another version of the conference has it that Mifflin told Washington boldly: "I am opposed to the revolution, and to all changes of government which occasion war and bloodshed."[65] If Mifflin said this, it seems not to have offended Washington for, as Armstrong noted, "The General gave them dinner . . . for which they seemed very thankful." When the delegates broached the subject of the Quaker exiles in Virginia, Washington explained that he had no authority to release them and suggested that they get in touch with the Pennsylvania officials "who had banished their friends."[66] In reporting to the Yearly Meeting afterward, the delegates insisted that

Gen. Washington and all the Officers then present, being a pretty many, were fully satisfied as to Friends Clearness and we hope and believe ... the Opportunity we had was useful many ways, there having been great Openness and many Observations upon various subjects to Edification and tending to remove and clear up some Prejudices which had been imbibed.[67]

Isaac Sharpless singled out Washington's courteous reception of the delegation as "abundant proof" of his good will toward the Quakers and added that "many a commander would have treated them with scant forbearance."[58]

Quaker writers have also been pleased by the hospitality which Washington extended to the wives of four of the exiles when they visited him in April, 1778, to seek his help in securing the release of the Winchester prisoners. Washington had already assured the ladies in writing of his willingness to assist them in their plan to send food, clothing, and medical supplies to the ailing prisoners; indeed, he had already interceded with Governor Wharton of Pennsylvania on their behalf.[69] But the four ladies—Mary Pemberton, Elizabeth Drinker, Susanna Jones, and Mary Pleasants—wished to discuss the plight of the prisoners with him personally, and without receiving authorization of any kind they left occupied Philadelphia and journeyed to his headquarters at Valley Forge. "We requested an audience with the General," Mrs. Drinker noted in her diary,

and sat with his wife, (a sociable, pretty kind of woman), until he came in. A number of officers were there who were very complaisant. ... It was not long before G. Washington came, and discoursed with us freely, but not so long as we could have wished, as dinner was served, to which he invited us. ... We had an elegant dinner, which was soon over, when we went out with ye Genls wife, up to her Chamber—and saw no more of him.[70]

Washington explained again that he had no jurisdiction over the Winchester prisoners, but he gave the ladies a pass to Lancaster, where they could press their suit before the state authorities. "As they seem much distressed," he wrote the governor, "humanity pleads strongly in their behalf."[71] When the ladies reached Lancaster, they learned to their joy that the prisoners had been released the day before.

Washington received many compliments, both at the time and afterward, for "the most cordial manner" in which he entertained his unexpected visitors. His amiable reception of the "four courageous Quaker women" is frequently offered as conclusive evidence that he did not share the animosity toward the Quakers prevailing among the patriots.[72] Even the exiles believed that Washington's sympathies were with them. When they reached his headquarters on their way back from Virginia, late in April, and requested and received permission to cross American lines into Philadelphia, "we esteemed it a proof," said one of the prisoners, "of the General's sense of justice and politeness."[73]

Washington's treatment of the Quakers during the Revolution has been accorded the highest praise by Quaker writers. "In all the relations of the General with the Friends," concluded Isaac Sharpless in his survey of the Society of Friends during the Revolution, "we find the greatest courtesy on his part, and the most respectful language, whether in minutes of meetings or in private letters on theirs. He understood their scruples and respected them, and they felt the reality of his politeness and sense of justice."[74] Sharpless certainly overstated the case; Washington did suspect the Quakers of "evil intentions" during the Pennsylvania campaign. Moreover, in 1781, he refused to permit a delegation of New England Friends to visit Quaker meetings on Long Island because of lingering suspicions about their intentions.[75] On the other hand, it is clear that Washington, as his prompt release of the Virginia draftees shows, was willing to respect the religious scruples of the Quakers against bearing arms during the Revolution. What he could not understand, however, was the insistence of Pennsylvania Quakers (who seem to have been more uncompromising than Quakers elsewhere) upon total abstention from the independence movement to which he was so passionately dedicated. They would not bear arms, of course, and Washington respected their religious scruples. But neither would they hold office under the Revolutionary government of Pennsylvania, affirm allegiance to it, pay its taxes, or even handle its paper money, and this Washington could not understand. Like most patriots, he wrongly concluded from the intransigence of Pennsylvania Friends that the Quakers wanted the British to win the war and perhaps were even secretly aiding them. Although, unlike many of the patriots, he strove to treat them with fairness and decency, he could never quite convince himself that they were not guilty of "evil intentions" toward the American cause. His forbearance, under these circumstances, is surely impressive, and Sharpless is doubtless correct in asserting that he "appreciated" the Quakers "far better than did those militant civilians, the Adamses of Massachusetts...."[76]

After the Revolution, Washington explained his attitude toward the Quakers to Brissot de Warville. "No person has spoken to me with more impartiality respecting the Quakers than General Washington...," reported Warville, who, like many Frenchmen, admired the Society of Friends for its antislavery activities.

He declared to me, that, in the course of the war, he had entertained an ill opinion of this society; he knew but little of them . . . and he attributed to their political sentiments, the effect of their religious principles. He told me, that having since known them better, he acquired an esteem for them; and that considering the simplicity of their manners, the purity of their morals, their exemplary economy and their attachment to the constitution, he considered this society as one of the best supports of the new government.[77]

Moreover, when Warner Mifflin sought him out, after he became President, to discuss slavery with him, he was treated with "kindness and respect" and reported afterward that Washington showed some understanding of Quaker policy during the Revolutionary War. "Mr. Mifflin," Washington asked at one point, "will you please to inform me on what principle you were opposed to the revolution?" "Yes, friend Washington," replied Mifflin, "upon the same principles that I should be opposed to a change in this government—all that ever was gained by revolutions are not an adequate compensation to the poor mangled soldier for the loss of life or limb." After a moment's pause, Washington declared: "Mr. Mifflin, I honor your sentiments; there is more in that than mankind have generally considered."[78]

Although Washington's associations, during the Revolution, with the Quakers—and with the Catholics and Universalists—showed that he was sensitive to the rights of conscience and "a total stranger to religious prejudices," only once, as Continental Commander, did he single out religious liberty, in a formal public statement, as one of the objectives for which the war was being fought. This was on November 16, 1782, when he was responding to a welcoming address made by the ministers, elders, and deacons of the Reformed

Protestant Dutch Church of Kingston, New York, on the occasion of his visit to the town. During the course of their address, the officers of the Kingston church declared that "our Religious Rights" were "partly involved in our Civil,"[79] and Washington, in his reply, declared:

Convinced that our Religious Liberties were as essential as our Civil, my endeavours have never been wanting to encourage and promote the one, while I have been contending for the other; and I am highly flattered by finding that my efforts have met the approbation of so respectable a body (Appendix, 4).

No doubt Washington had assumed all along that "Religious Rights" were involved in civil rights. In an address to the United Dutch Reformed churches of Hackensack and Schalenburg, New Jersey, shortly after the close of the war, he mentioned the "protection of our Civil and Religious Liberties" as one of the achievements of the Revolution (Appendix, 5). He also told the German Reformed congregation of New York City about the same time that the "establishment of Civil and Religious Liberty was the Motive which induced me to the field . . ." (Appendix, 6). If, on the whole, he had said little about this during the war, he had much to say publicly and of an explicit nature on the subject after he became President. In each case what he said grew out of some point raised in a formal address of congratulations similar to that delivered to him by the Kingston church.

After his inauguration as President on April 30, 1789, Washington received a veritable flood of congratulatory addresses from towns, cities, colleges, state legislatures, fraternal organizations, and from religious bodies, to each of which he was expected to make a formal acknowledgment.

Wherever he went, there were the inevitable complimentary speeches and polite replies. Washington must have become heartily tired of these occasions; in fact, he once hinted that he would not mind if his felicitators "would bring an answer" along with their addresses.[80]

Among these many exchanges of compliments were twenty-two with the major religious bodies of his day. There is, as one would expect, much in the addresses of these groups and in Washington's responses of a ceremonial, platitudinous, and even pompous nature. The addresses were, as the Virginia Baptists put it, largely "shouts of congratulations" upon Washington's elevation to the highest office in the land.[81] They consisted of praise for Washington's services in both war and peace, pledges of loyal support for the new national government, expressions of hope for the flourishing of religion and morality in the new nation, and invocations of divine blessings upon the President. Washington's replies, for their part, were properly modest as regards himself, expressed gratification at the professions of loyalty to the federal government, and, as regards religion, frequently consisted of little more than paraphrases of what had been said by his congratulators. Nevertheless, there is also much that is valuable in these exchanges for the insight which they give us into Washington's views both on the subject of religious freedom and on the question of the relation between church and state in the young republic.

In thirteen of the twenty-two exchanges there are direct references to religious liberty. Three of the references are largely conventional in nature. When the Synod of the Dutch Reformed church, for example, pointed out that "just government protects all in their religious rights,"[82] Washington said simply that he "readily" agreed with this sentiment (Appendix, 14). Similarly, when the Methodists praised Washington's concern for the "preservation of those civil and religious liberties which have been transmitted to us by . . . the glorious revolution,"* Washington assured them of his "desires to contribute whatever may be in my power towards the preservation of the civil and religious liberties of the American People" (Appendix, 10). In the same manner, when responding to a statement by John Murray on behalf of the Universalists that "the peculiar doctrine which we hold is . . . friendly to the order and happiness of Society,"[83] Washington merely voiced his hope that citizens of every faith would enjoy "the auspicious years of Peace, liberty and free enquiry, with which they are now favored" (Appendix, 23). More interesting, perhaps, is Washington's response to felicitations from the General Convention of the Protestant Episcopal church meeting in Philadelphia. When the Episcopalians, during the course of their long letter, expressed pleasure at the "election of a civil Ruler . . . who has happily united a tender regard for other churches with an inviolable attachment to his own,"[84] Washington seized the opportunity to remark:

It affords edifying prospects indeed to see Christians of different denominations dwell together in more charity, and conduct themselves in respect to each other with a more christian-like spirit than ever they have done in any former age, or in any other Nation (Appendix, 13).

*The English Methodist, Dr. Thomas Coke, joined Francis Asbury in presenting the address of American Methodists personally to Washington, and the reference to the "glorious revolution" occasioned considerable embarrassment for him upon his return to England. (Paul F. Boller, Jr., "George Washington and the Methodists," *Historical Magazine of the Protestant Episcopal Church*, XXVIII [June, 1959], 165-86).

The Baptists of Virginia were far less confident than Washington that a spirit of charity prevailed among the different denominations of the country. They had not forgotten the discrimination they had suffered before the Revolution, and they had serious doubts as to whether the new federal Constitution satisfactorily safeguarded religious liberty for everyone. They took their correspondence with Washington, therefore, with the utmost seriousness. At a meeting of the General Committee of Baptists in Virginia in March, 1788, the question was raised: "Does the new Federal Constitution, which has now lately made its appearance in public, make sufficient provision for the secure enjoyment of religious liberty?" After considerable discussion and a careful reading of the Constitution, the question was put to a vote and decided unanimously in the negative. A committee, headed by John Leland, was then appointed to prepare an address to Washington on the subject and to secure the co-operation of Baptists in other states in seeking amendments to the Constitution. The address, prepared by Leland, was adopted at the annual meeting of the General Committee at Richmond in May the following year and transmitted to Washington at some undetermined date after the close of the meeting.[85] "When the Constitution first made its appearance in Virginia," the Baptists told Washington in this document,

we, as a society, had unusual strugglings of mind; fearing that the *liberty of conscience,* dearer to us than property or life, was not sufficiently secured—Perhaps our jealousies were heightened on account of the usage that we received under the royal government, when Mobs, Bonds, Fines, and Prisons were our frequent attendants.—Convinced on one hand that without an effective national government we should fall into disunion and all the consequent evils; and on the other fearing that we should be accessary to some religious oppression, should any one Society in the Union preponderate over all the rest. But amidst all the inquietudes of mind, our consolation arose from this consideration "The plan must be good for it bears the signature of a tried, trusty friend"—and if religious liberty is rather insecure, "The administration will certainly prevent all oppression for a Washington will preside." . . . Should the horrid evils of faction, ambition, war, perfidy, fraud and persecution, for conscience sake, which have been so pestiferous in Asia and Europe, ever approach the borders of our happy nation, may the name and administration of our beloved *President,* like the radiant source of day, drive all those dark clouds from the American hemisphere.[86]

In his reply, Washington praised the Baptists as "firm friends to civil liberty" and as "persevering Promoters of our glorious revolution" and tried to quiet their fears about the Constitution.

If I could have entertained the slightest apprehension that the Constitution framed in the Convention, where I had the honor to preside, might possibly endanger the religious rights of any ecclesiastical Society, certainly I would never have placed my signature to it; and if I could now conceive that the general Government might ever be so administered as to render the liberty of conscience insecure, I beg you will be persuaded that no one would be more zealous than myself to establish effectual barriers against the horrors of spiritual tyranny, and every species of religious persecution—For you, doubtless, remember that I have often expressed my sentiments, that every man, conducting himself as a good citizen, and being accountable to God alone for his religious opinions, ought to be protected in worshipping the Deity according to the dictates of his own conscience (Appendix, 8).

Baptist writers have united in applauding Washington's expression of views on this occasion. They have been especially fond of his phrase, "effectual barriers against the horrors of spiritual tyranny," which some of them look upon as the forerunner of Jefferson's "wall of separation between church and state." "Both loved figures of speech," declared Henry Moehlman; "Washington, the military man, thought of 'barriers;' Jefferson, the man of home life, thought of a substantial, separating, secure wall around his estate. A barrier is the equivalent of a wall, especially when it is 'effectual.' "[87]

Baptist historians have also regarded the correspondence of the Virginia Baptists with Washington as a major event in the campaign for a federal Bill of Rights. They have even suggested that the inclusion of a religious-liberty provision in the First Amendment "resulted from what might have seemed the extreme sensitiveness of the Virginia Baptist General Committee."[88] There was, of course, no such direct relationship between the Baptist exchange with Washington and the formulation of the First Amendment. The Baptists were not the only ones pressing for religious-liberty guarantees in the Constitution at this time. Besides, it was James Madison, not Washington, who took the lead in drafting and introducing the Bill of Rights amendments in the first Congress. Nevertheless, American Baptists generally, and Virginia Baptists in particular, played a prominent part in the agitation for a federal Bill of Rights. There is also evidence that it was Madison who first suggested that the Virginia Baptists correspond with Washington on the subject of religious liberty.[89] Some months after he had introduced his amendments in Congress, Madison informed Washington: "One of the principal leaders of the Baptists [probably John Leland] lately sent me word that the amendments had entirely satisfied the disaffected of his sect and that it would appear in their subsequent conduct."[90]

Several months after the exchange of views with the Virginia Baptists, Washington had occasion to spell out his ideas on liberty of conscience at greater length in a speech which he made to the Quakers. Philadelphia Quakers, seeking a "formal reconciliation" with the new government, joined with New York Friends in sending a delegation to New York in October, 1789, to read to Washington a statement prepared by the Philadelphia Yearly Meeting.[91] The Quakers began by assuring Washington of their affection for him personally and of their loyalty to the federal Constitution. Then they got to the heart of the matter:

The free toleration which the citizens of these States enjoy in the public worship of the Almighty, agreeable to the dictates of their consciences, we esteem among the choicest of blessings; and as we desire to be filled with fervent charity for those who differ from us in matters of faith or practice ... so we trust we may justly claim it from others. And on a full persuasion that the divine principles we profess lead into harmony and concord, we can take no part in carrying on war, on any occasion or under any power; but are bound in conscience to lead quiet and peaceable lives in godliness and honesty. ...

Still, apparently, rankling from the charges of treason that had been hurled at them during the Revolution, the Quakers assured Washington they had never been involved, "from our first establishment as a religious society, with fomenting or countenancing tumults or conspiracies. ..."[92]

In his friendly response, Washington gently, but frankly, took exception, in passing, to Quaker pacifism. At the same time he stated his position on the rights of conscience in religious matters with precision and clarity:

Government being, among other purposes, instituted to protect the persons and consciences of men from oppression, it certainly is the duty of rulers, not only to abstain from it themselves, but, according to their stations, to prevent it in others. The liberty enjoyed by the people of these States, of worshipping Almighty God agreeably to their consciences, is not only among the choicest of their blessings, but also of their rights. While men perform their social duties faithfully, they do all that society or the state can with propriety demand or expect; and remain responsible only to their Maker for the religion, or modes of faith, which they may prefer or profess.

Your principles and conduct are well known to me; and it is doing the people called Quakers no more than justice to say, that (except their declining to share with others the burthen of the common defence) there is no denomination among us, who are more exemplary and useful citizens.

I assure you very explicitly, that in my opinion the conscientious scruples of all men should be treated with great delicacy and tendernes; and it is my wish and desire, that the laws may always be as extensively accomodated to them, as a due regard to the protection and essential interests of the nation may justify and permit (Appendix, 16).

While the Quakers, as pacifists, could not agree fully with the balance which Washington struck between the rights of conscience and the "essential interests of the nation," they were delighted with the great respect which he accorded the "conscientious scruples of all men" as well as with the high regard which he expressed for them as citizens. The delegation "was very much pleased with his behaviour," Susanna Dilwyn wrote afterward; "indeed he gains the esteem of everybody—those who agree with few other things all unite in admiring General Washington."[93] In France, the *Patriote Français,* in a sympathetic account of the exchange, called attention to Washington's praise of the Quakers as "useful and exemplary" and expressed the hope that Washington's attitude would "close the mouth of the slanderers of the Quakers."[94] And, indeed, Quaker historians generally agree that Washington's public "appreciation of Quakers" at this time helped to dissolve the animosities toward the Society of Friends that still lingered from the Revolutionary period.[95]

In March, 1790, when the Free Quakers (a group of Quakers who had been disowned by the orthodox Friends for supporting the Revolutionary war and had formed their own nonpacifist society in 1781) sent Washington a long congratulatory message in which they commented critically on the pacifist policy of the Society of Friends, Washington firmly declined to become involved in the dispute between the two organizations:

... Having always considered the conscientious scruples of religious belief as resting entirely with the sects that profess, or the individuals who entertain them, I cannot, consistent with this uniform sentiment, otherwise notice the circumstances referred to in your address, than by adding the tribute of my acknowledgement, to that of our country, for those services which the members of your particular community rendered to the common cause in the course of our revolution. ... (Appendix, 18).

If the Baptists and the Quakers were particularly interested in liberty of conscience under the new Constitution, there were other religionists who deplored the omission of any reference to deity in the document. The Constitution is, in fact, completely secular in nature. But the story that Alexander Hamilton, after the Constitutional Convention, was asked by a Presbyterian clergyman "why some suitable recognition of the Almighty had not been placed in the

Constitution" and replied, "I declare we forgot it," has no basis in fact.[96] Indeed, Luther Martin, who refused to sign the Constitution and opposed ratification, insisted afterward that "some members" of the convention were "so unfashionable" as to want an acknowledgment of the Almighty included in the document. The Constitution-makers were by no means hostile to organized religion, but they were undoubtedly eager to avoid embroiling the new government in religious controversies. The clause prohibiting religious tests for officeholding was adopted, as Martin acknowledged, "by a great majority of the convention and without much debate" and it was certainly welcomed by fervent church-state separationists like the Baptists.[97] Presbyterians in northern New England, however, were somewhat less enthusiastic about this constitutional aloofness from religion. In October, 1789, when Washington was traveling in New England, the ministers and elders of the first Presbytery of the Eastward (composed of Presbyterian churches in northeastern Massachusetts and in New Hampshire) sent him a long welcoming address from Newburyport in which they commented in some detail on the Constitution. They had no objection, they declared, to "the want of *a religious test*, that grand engine of persecution in every tyrant's hand." Moreover, they praised Washington for his toleration in religious matters:

The catholic spirit breathed in all your public acts supports us in the pleasing assurance that no religious establishments—no exclusive privileges tending to elevate one denomination of Christians to the depression of the rest, shall ever be ratified by the signature of the *President* during your administration. On the contrary we bless God that your whole deportment bids all denominations confidently to expect to find in you the watchful guardian of their equal liberties. . . .

Nevertheless, they continued, "we should not have been alone in rejoicing to have seen some explicit acknowledgment of the *only true God and Jesus Christ, whom he hath sent* inserted some where in the *Magna Charta* of our country."[98]

Washington's reply was a clear statement of his views on the relation between church and state under the new Constitution. After thanking the Presbytery for its "affectionate welcome," he declared:

And here, I am persuaded, you will permit me to observe, that the path of true piety is so plain as to require but little political attention. To this consideration we ought to ascribe the absence of any regulation respecting religion from the Magna Charta of our country.

To the guidance of the ministers of the gospel this important object is, perhaps, more properly committed. It will be your care to instruct the ignorant, to reclaim the devious; and in the progress of morality and science, to which our government will give every furtherance, we may expect confidently, the advancement of true religion and the completion of happiness[99] (Appendix, 17).

Washington's response was tactfully phrased, as were all his responses to addresses of religious organizations, but there is every reason to believe that the policy of "friendly separation" which he enunciated here represented his own considered opinions and those of most of his associates in the Constitutional Convention.

Not all Americans agreed with the Eastward Presbytery in regarding religious tests as "that grand engine of persecution in every tyrant's hand." Many of the states continued, as in the colonial period, to restrict officeholding to Protestants in the constitutions which they adopted during the Revolutionary period. Moreover, there was some grumbling about the omission of religious tests in the federal Constitution on the ground that the national government might fall under the control of Roman Catholics, Jews, and infidels.[100] One writer even warned that there was "a very serious danger, that the pope of Rome might be elected President." Probably few people took such talk seriously. Most Americans (who had come to esteem their Catholic fellow-citizens during the Revolution) undoubtedly shared James Iredell's impatience with such absurd warnings. "A native American," he declared with some irritation in the North Carolina ratifying convention,

must have very singular good fortune who, after residing fourteen years in his own country, should come to Europe, enter Romish orders, obtain the promotion of cardinal, afterward that of Pope, and at length be so much in the confidence of his country as to be elected President. It would be still more extraordinary, if he should give up his popedom for our presidency.[101]

Nevertheless, a few days after Washington's inauguration an article appeared on page one of the *Gazette of the United States* (New York), insisting that the foundations of the American republic had been laid by the Protestant religion and that Protestants therefore deserved special consideration under the federal government.[102] In a long letter to the *Gazette* the following month, Father John Carroll vigorously challenged this point of view. "Every friend to the rights of conscience," he declared, "must have felt pain" at this evidence of "religious intolerance." "Perhaps," he continued, the writer

is one of those who think it consistent with justice to exclude certain citizens from the honors and emoluments of society merely on account of their religious opinions, provided they be not restrained by racks and forfeitures from the exercise of that worship which their consciences approve. If such be his views, in vain then have Americans associated into one great national Union, under the firm persuasion that they were to retain, when associated, every natural right not expressly surrendered.

Pointing out that the "blood of Catholics flowed as freely" as that of "any of their fellow citizens" during the Revolution and that American Catholics had "concurred with perhaps greater unanimity than any other body of men" in the work of the Constitutional Convention, Father Carroll concluded: ". . . the establishment of the American empire was not the work of this or that religion, but arose from the exertion of all her citizens to redress their wrongs, to assert their rights, and lay its foundation on the soundest principles of justice and equal liberty."[103] It is not surprising that American Catholics, like the Virginia Baptists, looked upon the friendly sentiments which Washington expressed to them a few months later in response to their congratulatory address as of major importance in the development of religious toleration in the new nation.

The address, signed by John Carroll and presented to Washington on March 15, 1790, by Charles Carroll of Carrollton, Daniel Carroll, Thomas FitzSimons, Dominick Lynch, and Rev. Nicholas Burke of St. Peter's Church in New York City, emphasized the influence which Washington, by his "example as well as by vigilance," had on the "manners of our fellow-citizens." Calling attention to the progress of the United States under Washington's leadership, the address went on to say:

From these happy events, in which none can feel a warmer interest than ourselves, we derive additional pleasure by recollecting, that you, Sir, have been the principal instrument to effect so rapid a change in our political situation. This prospect of national prosperity is peculiarly pleasing to us on another account; because whilst our country preserves her freedom and independence, we shall have a well founded title to claim from her justice equal rights of citizenship, as the price of our blood spilt under your eyes, and of our common exertions for her defense, under your auspicious conduct, rights rendered more dear to us by the remembrance of former hardships. When we pray for the preservation of them, where they have been granted; and expect the full extension of them from the justice of those States, which still restrict them; when we solicit the protection of Heaven over our common country; we neither omit nor can omit recommending your preservation to the singular care of divine providence. . . .[104]

Washington's reply, it has been noted, was partly addressed to "the great non-Catholic population of the nation."[105] "As mankind become more liberal," Washington said,

they will be more apt to allow, that all those who conduct themselves as worthy members of the community, are equally entitled to the protection of civil government. I hope ever to see America among the foremost nations in examples of justice and liberality. And I presume that your fellow-citizens will not forget the patriotic part which you took in the accomplishment of their revolution, and the establishment of their government; or the important assistance which they received from a nation in which the Roman Catholic religion is professed (Appendix, 19).

He concluded by wishing the Catholics "every temporal and spiritual felicity." Washington's statement, according to Thomas O'Gorman, "is among the classics of the land and one of its most precious heirlooms."[106] Peter Guilday called it "this precious document" and added: "Washington's reply has brought joy to the hearts of all American Catholics since that time; but it was especially to the Catholics of 1790 that the encomium of the first President meant much in the way of patience and encouragement."[107] Later that year Washington's exchange with the Catholics was published in London with the prefatory comment:

The following address from the Roman Catholics, which was copied from the American News papers—whilst it breathes fidelity to the States which protect them, asserts, with decency, the common-rights of mankind; and the answer of the President truly merits that esteem, which his liberal sentiments, mild administration, and prudent justice have obtained him. . . . Is this not a lesson? Britons remain intolerant and inexorable to the claims of sound policy and of nature. . . . Britons, view and blush![108]

Like the Catholics, American Jews were also eager that the rights guaranteed all Americans under the federal Constitution be made a reality for citizens of Jewish faith. There were probably less than three thousand Jews in the United States when Washington became President.[109] During the colonial period, Jewish settlers in America had at first encountered much of the same kind of discrimination and legal restrictions that they had been accustomed to in Europe for centuries past. Nevertheless, by the time of the American Revolution, as Oscar Handlin has pointed out, they had gradually won civil, political, and religious rights that far exceeded anything that their fellow-religionists in Europe enjoyed, even in Holland.[110] Like the Catholics, American Jews realized that their future was intimately involved in the achievement of the liberal ideals proclaimed in the Declaration of Independence, and the majority gave their warm support to the Revolutionary cause. They also heartily endorsed the work of the Constitutional Convention and rejoiced especially that religious tests for officeholding (which still existed in most of the thirteen states) were prohibited in the federal Constitution. There were, at the time of the adoption of the Constitution, six Jewish congregations in the United States: Shearith Israel, the oldest, in New York City; Jeshuat Israel (now Touro Synagogue) in Newport, Rhode Island; Mikveh Israel in Philadelphia; Beth Elohim in Charleston, South Carolina; Mikveh Israel in Savannah, Georgia; and Beth Shalome in Richmond, Virginia.

Early in 1790, Shearith Israel in New York began making plans for a joint address to Washington by all six congregations pledging support to the new federal government and expressing gratitude for "the Enfranchisement which is secured to us *Jews* by the Federal Constitution."[111] But the slowness of communications between the six cities, together with the reluctance of the Newport congregation to participate ("as we are so small in number, it would be treating the Legislature & other large bodies in this State, with a great degree of indelicacy, for us to address the President ... previous to any of them"),[112] produced so many delays that the Savannah Jews finally decided to go ahead on their own. On May 6, 1790, Levi Sheftall, president of the Savannah congregation, sent a letter to Washington on behalf of Mikveh Israel which declared in part:

Your unexampled liberality and extensive philanthropy have dispelled that cloud of bigotry and superstition which has long, as a veil, shaded religion—unrivetted the fetters of enthusiasm—enfranchised us with all the privileges and immunities of free citizens, and initiated us into the grand mass of legislative mechanism.[113]

"I rejoice," Washington replied, in what has been called "gracious and flowing diction,"[114]

that a spirit of liberality and philanthropy is much more prevalent than it formerly was among the enlightened nations of the earth; and that your brethren will benefit thereby in proportion as it shall become still more extensive. Happily the people of the United States have, in many instances, exhibited examples worthy of imitation—The salutary influence of which will doubtless extend much farther. . . . May the same wonder-working Deity, who long since delivering the Hebrews from their Egyptian oppressors planted them in the promised land . . . still continue to water them with the dews of Heaven and to make the inhabitants of every denomination participate in the temporal and spiritual blessings of that people whose God is Jehovah (Appendix, 20).

Somewhat annoyed that the Savannah congregation had acted independently ("We do not by any means, conceive ourselves well treated by the Georgians"),[115] Shearith Israel renewed its efforts in June for united action by the other five congregations, explaining, in a circular letter, that "we are led to understand that mode will be less irksome to the president than troubling him to reply to every individual address."[116] This time Jeshuat Israel in Newport agreed to co-operate ("notwithstanding our reluctance of becoming the primary addressers from this State")[117] and insisted only that Shearith Israel prepare an address in which "your sentiments will be properly express'd & *unequivocally,* relative to the Enfranchisement which is secured to us *Jews* by the Federal Constitution."[118] Beth Elohim in Charleston also approved joint action and submitted the draft of an address which it had prepared for possible use by Shearith Israel. In this address, which was never utilized, Washington was linked with "Moses, Joshua, Othniel, Gideon, Samuel,

David, Maccabeus and other holy men of old, who were raised up by God, for the deliverance of our nation, His people, from their oppression."[119]

By August, however, Shearith Israel, for some unaccountable reason, had still not acted. Learning that Washington was planning a trip to Rhode Island that month and that the state legislature and King David's Lodge of Masons intended to deliver welcoming addresses, Jeshuat Israel, impatient of any further delay, composed what David de Sola Pool has called a "historic address" of its own for presentation to the President while he was in Newport.[120] Jeshuat Israel's exchange with Washington, the most famous of the three exchanges which American Jews had with the President, took place on August 17, 1790. The Newport congregation began by formally welcoming Washington to the city and then declared:

Deprived as we have hitherto been of the invaluable rights of free citizens, we now ... behold a Government which to bigotry gives no sanction, to persecution no assistance—but generously affording to All liberty of conscience, and immunities of citizenship—deeming everyone, of whatever nation, tongue, or language equal parts of the great governmental machine. . . . For all the blessings of civil and religious liberty which we enjoy under an equal and benign administration we desire to send up our thanks to the Antient of days. . . .[121]

In his reply, which he read in person, Washington repeated the "punch line"[122] ("a Government which to bigotry gives no sanction, to persecution no assistance") of the congregation's address, as he was accustomed to do on such occasions, but he also emphasized the important point that religious freedom is something more than mere toleration.

"The Citizens of the United States of America," he told the
Newport Jews,

have a right to applaud themselves for having given to Mankind
examples of an enlarged and liberal policy, a policy worthy of
imitation. All possess alike liberty of conscience and immunities
of citizenship. It is now no more that toleration is spoken of, as
if it was by the indulgence of one class of people, that another
enjoyed the exercise of their inherent natural rights. For happily
the Government of the United States, which gives to bigotry no
sanction, to persecution no assistance, requires only that they
who live under its protection should demean themselves as good
citizens, in giving it on all occasions their effectual support....
May the children of the Stock of Abraham, who dwell in this
land, continue to merit and enjoy the good will of the other
inhabitants, while every one shall sit in safety under his own vine
and fig tree, and there shall be none to make him afraid (Appendix, 21).

Washington's statement, which has been called "immortal"[123] and "memorable,"[124] naturally delighted the Newport
congregation and the Jewish congregations elsewhere in the
United States. It has, moreover, justifiably been highly prized
by later generations of American Jews. Dr. Morris A. Gutstein
characterized it as one of the "most outstanding expressions
on religious liberty and equality in America"[125] and insisted
that it "will be quoted by every generation in which religious
liberty is cherished."[126] Dr. David de Sola Pool maintained
that Washington made a "classic definition of American
democracy" when he stressed the primacy of "inherent
natural rights" over toleration.[127] Harry Golden said that
Washington "articulated his divine destiny" as a champion
of "inalienable rights" in his exchange with the Newport
Jews.[128] For Harry Simonhoff, Washington's statement "ranks

with the best of Hamilton or Jefferson." "Neither philo-semitic nor anti-semitic," he adds,

the "Father of his country" seeks impartially to secure for Jews the rights of human beings. Yet he goes a step further. The probable recollection of Jewish contributions to the war effort causes him to show annoyance at the word toleration when applied to freedom of worship. One cannot but detect compassion, or even anxiety in his letter to the Newport congregation. . . .[129]

Simonhoff (like Harry Golden, who says that Washington's statement "came out of sad and solitary communion")[130] is doubtless reading too much into Washington's remarks on this occasion. Still, the effect of Washington's address, as Benjamin Hartogensis suggested many years ago, "could not have been other than to arouse strongly the feeling of the people of Rhode Island for the Jews."[131]

Because of the independent action taken by Mikveh Israel and Jeshuat Israel, the New York congregation's plans for a joint address of all six Jewish congregations failed of realization. But late in 1790, when the federal capital was being transferred from New York to Philadelphia, the remaining four congregations succeeded in uniting to present their compliments to Washington shortly after his arrival in the new capital. Arranged by the Philadelphia congregation, with the concurrence of the congregations in New York, Charleston, and Richmond, the final exchange with Washington took place on December 13, 1790. Matthew Josephson, president of Mikveh Israel, presented the congratulations of the four congregations to Washington in person. The address began by expressing affection for Washington's "character and Person" and praising him for his great services to his country in "the late glorious revolution." It went on:

But not to your sword alone is our present happiness to be ascribed; That indeed opened the way to the reign of freedom, but never was it perfectly secure, till your hand gave birth to the federal constitution, and you renounced the joys of retirement to seal by your administration in peace, what you had atchieved in war.[132]

In his response, Washington again expressed his warm regard for his Jewish fellow-citizens and applauded the fact that the "liberal sentiment towards each other which marks every political and religious denomination of men in this country stands unrivalled in the history of nations. . . ." (Appendix, 24)

Washington's replies to the three Jewish addresses have been deeply cherished by American Jews in the nineteenth and twentieth centuries. Jewish historians commonly regard them as "of great historic interest as well as of importance." "For a century and a half," declared Morris W. Schappes a few years ago, "these declarations have been used to confound the enemy in the ceaseless struggle against those who would subvert American ideals through the propagation of anti-Semitism and other doctrines of bigotry."[133] "These three letters of Washington," according to Lee M. Friedman,

deserve to rank with the Constitutional interpretations of Chief Justice Marshall and of Alexander Hamilton's *Federalist*. As if issuing an Emancipation Proclamation, Washington rose to the opportunity which the addresses from these Jewish congregations afforded. He gave point to the theory of American democracy which, finally and expressly embodied in the Bill of Rights, struck from the Jews of the United States the shackles of disabilities, survivals of the past in other lands, handicapping them politically and restricting them in the enjoyment of their religion. Too little known to the general public, these letters stand enshrined in a place of honor in American Jewish history.[134]

In 1876, delegates to a convention of the Union of American Hebrew Congregations made a special trip to Mount Vernon to do honor to Washington's memory. Isaac M. Wise planted a tree near Washington's tomb, Lewis Abraham read the correspondence between Washington and the Jewish congregations to the assembled delegates, and Simon Wolf pointed out in his address to the group that this correspondence had been translated into Hebrew and "had aroused much interest in Europe and Asia."[135]

Washington's Newport statement, in particular, with its emphasis on "inherent natural rights" and its inclusion of the phrase, "to bigotry no sanction," has, as Lee Friedman observes, become "famous in American Jewish history."[136] Historians of American Judaism have uniformly regarded it as a "classic document"[137] in the development of freedom in the United States and have praised not only its content but its "beautiful" and "impressive" style as well.[138] Indeed, in an excess of enthusiasm, one writer even suggested that it "bears unmistakable signs of having been originally composed in Rabbinical Hebrew."[139]

In 1824, while championing a bill in the Maryland legislature for removing all political restrictions from Jewish citizens of the state, Colonel J. W. D. Worthington read Washington's exchange with the Newport congregation *in toto* to show that "the father of his country was in favour of the political equality of the Israelites. . . ."[140] Grover Cleveland and other notables also made extensive use of this exchange in speeches which they delivered in New York City in November, 1905, in commemoration of the 250th anniversary of the settlement of the Jews in America.[141] And in 1908, when a memorial tablet was unveiled in the

Newport synagogue, Leon Huhner read Washington's Newport statement at the end of his dedicatory address and voiced
the hope that the first President's views "may be repeated
anew in the same spirit, by the entire community, in every
generation."[142]

With the rise of the Nazi terror in the 1930's, Washington's exchange with the Newport synagogue took on renewed
significance for American Jews. In August, 1940, the 150th
anniversary of Washington's Newport address was celebrated by Jewish congregations in Newport and in New
York. In a series of nationally broadcast speeches delivered
for the occasion in the Central Synagogue in New York
City, Rabbi Jonah M. Wise contrasted Washington, the man
of "truth, faith, and liberty" with the "leering, brutal
conquerors of Europe"; Dr. Morris A. Gutstein emphasized
Washington's distinction between "two types of liberty:
one, mere *Toleration*, another, real *Equality*"; and Dr. David
de Sola Pool called attention to Washington's "utter freedom
from religious prejudice, and his conviction that in this new
America all religions must stand on a footing of equality."[143]

The following year, when the American Jewish Committee published an analysis of anti-Semitic propaganda in
the United States, it reproduced Washington's Newport
address on the first page of the pamphlet and entitled the
report *To Bigotry No Sanction*.[144] The famous phrase—
"Happily the Government of the United States ... gives to
bigotry no sanction, to persecution no assistance"—was also
inscribed on the pedestal of the monument erected in Chi-
cago in December, 1941, to the memory of Haym Salomon,
the Jewish financier who contributed so much to the Revolutionary cause.[145] It also appears on the tablet which was

placed on the southern wall of the Newport synagogue when it became a national historic site in the summer of 1947.[146]

Two years after his exchange with the American Jewish congregations, Washington had a brief encounter with a little group of Swedenborgians in Maryland. In January, 1793, when he was visiting Baltimore, the tiny New Church Society, which had been organized in the city the previous year, "boldly" (as the historian of the movement puts it)[147] presented him with a copy of Emanuel Swedenborg's *The True Christian Religion,* together with an "energetic"[148] address rejoicing that "Priestcraft and Kingcraft, those banes of human felicity, are hiding their diminished heads" and that "equality in State, as well as in Church, proportionably to merit, are considered the true criterion of the majesty of the people."[149] In what Swedenborgian writers regard as a "rational" and "manly" reply,[150] Washington paid tribute to freedom of religion and then added significantly: "In this enlightened age & in this Land of equal liberty it is our boast, that a man's religious tenets will not forfeit the protection of the Laws, nor deprive him of the right of attaining & holding the highest offices that are known in the United States" (Appendix, 27). It was Washington's final public insistence upon "real *Equality*" rather than "mere *Toleration*" for citizens of every faith in the young republic.

In September, 1796, Washington issued his Farewell Address to the nation. The "wisdom of Providence," he declared, in a passage reminiscent of the notes he had jotted down at the beginning of his presidency, "has ordained that men, on the same subjects, shall not always think alike." Nevertheless, "charity and benevolence when they happen to differ," he continued, "may so far shed their benign influence as to banish those invectives which proceed from illiberal prejudices and jealousies."[151] A few months later, in responding to the address of the twenty-four Philadelphia clergymen on the occasion of his retirement from office, he expressed his "unspeakable pleasure" at viewing the

harmony and brotherly love which characterize the Clergy of different denominations, as well in this, as in other parts of the United States; exhibiting to the world a new and interesting spectacle, at once the pride of our country and the surest basis of universal harmony (Appendix, 29).

The Philadelphia clergymen doubtless realized that Washington himself had played a leading role in producing this "new and interesting spectacle." He had labored hard, while he was President, as well as during the Revolution, to banish "illiberal prejudices and jealousies" in religious matters from the nation and to throw his weight against the "power of bigotry and superstition" in the young republic. It is of course too much to say, as did the so-called "Shaker Bible," published in 1808, that "the wise and generous Washington" was solely responsible for the achievement of "civil and religious liberty" and the "rights of conscience" in the United States.[152] Still, by the example he set, in word and deed, as Continental Commander and as President, Washington unquestionably deserves major credit, along with Jefferson and Madison, for establishing the ideals of religious liberty and freedom of conscience (without which there can be no genuine cultural and intellectual freedom) for Protestants, Catholics, and Jews—and for Deists and freethinkers as well—firmly in the American tradition.

APPENDIX

Letters and Addresses by Washington
To Religious Organizations

1

To the Ministers, Elders, & Deacons of the Dutch Reformed Church at Raritan [New York].

[June 2, 1779]

GENTLEMEN

To meet the approbation of good men cannot but be agreeable. Your affectionate expressions make it still more so.

In quartering an army, and in supplying its wants, distress and inconvenience will often occur to the Citizen. I feel myself happy in a consciousness that these have been strictly limited by necessity and in your opinion of my attention to the rights of my fellow Citizens.

I thank you Gentlemen sincerely for the sense you entertain of the conduct of the Army; and for the Interest you take in my welfare. I trust the goodness of the cause and the exertions of the People under Divine Protection will give us that honourable Peace for which we are contending. Suffer me Gentlemen to wish the reformed Church at Raritan a long continuance of its present Minister & consistory and all the blessings which flow from piety & Religion.

I am &c

G. WASHINGTON.

(Papers of George Washington, Library of Congress, CCCCXCV, 400.)

163

2

To the Reverend the Minister, the Elders and Deacons of the reformed Protestant Dutch Church in the City of Albany.

June 28, 1782

GENTLEMEN

I am extremely happy in this opportunity of blending my public duty with my private satisfaction, by paying a due attention to the Frontiers and advanced Posts of this State and at the same time visiting this antient & respectable City of Albany.

While I consider the approbation of the wise and the virtuous, as the highest possible reward for my services, I beg you will be assured, Gentlemen, that I now experience the most sensible pleasure from the favourable sentiments you are pleased to express of my Conduct.

Your benevolent wishes & fervent prayers for my personal welfare and felicity, demand all my gratitude. May the preservation of your civil and religious Liberties still be the care of an indulgent Providence; and may the rapid increase and universal extension of knowledge virtue and true Religion be the consequence of a speedy and honourable Peace.

I am Gentlemen &c

G. WASHINGTON

(Papers, CCCCXCV, 336-37.)

3

To the Ministers Elders and Deacons of the reformed Protestant Dutch Church of the Town of Schenectady.

June 30, 1782

GENTLEMEN

I sincerely thank you for your congratulations on my arrival in this place.

Whilst I join in adoring that supreme being to whom alone can be attributed the signal successes of our Arms, I cannot but express gratitude to you for so distinguished a testemony of your regard.

May the same Providence that has hitherto, in so remarkable a manner Envinced the justice of our cause, lead us to a speedy and honorable peace, and may its attendant Blessings soon restore this once flourishing Town to its former Prosperity.

G. WASHINGTON

(Papers, CCCCXCV, 338.)

4

To the Ministers, Elders and Deacons of the reformed Protestant Dutch Church at Kingston

November 16, 1782

GENTLEMEN

I am happy in receiving this public mark of the Esteem of the Ministers, Elders and Deacons of the reformed Protestant Dutch Church in Kingston.

Convinced that our Religious Liberties were as essential as our Civil, my endeavours have never been wanting to encourage and promote the one, while I have been contending for the other; and I am highly flattered by finding that my efforts have met the approbation of so respectable a body.

In return for your kind concern for my temporal and eternal happiness, permit me to assure you that my wishes are reciprocal; and that you may be enabled to hand down your Religion pure and undefiled to a posterity worthy of their Ancestors.

I am Gentlemen

Yours &c

G. WASHINGTON

(Papers, CCCXCV, 382-83.)

5

To the Ministers, Elders, and Deacons of the Two United Dutch Reformed Churches of Hackensack and Schalenburg and the Inhabitants of Hackensack

November 10, 1783

GENTN.: Your affectionate congratulations on the happy conclusion of the War, and the glorious prospect now opening to this extensive Country, cannot but be extremely satisfactory to me.

Having shared in common, the hardships and dangers of the War with my virtuous fellow Citizens in the field, as well as with those who on the Lines have been immediately exposed to the Arts and Arms of the Enemy, I feel the most lively sentiments of gratitude to that divine Providence which has graciously interposed for the protection of our Civil and Religious Liberties.

In retireing from the field of Contest to the sweets of private life, I claim no merit, but if in that retirement my most earnest wishes and prayers can be of any avail, nothing will exceed the prosperity of our common Country, and the temporal and spiritual felicity of those who are represented in your Address.

(Fitzpatrick, *The Writings of George Washington*, XXVII, 239-40.)

6

To the Minister[,] Elders, Deacons & Members of the reformed German Congregation in the City of New York.

[November 27, 1783]

GENTLEMEN,

The illustrious and happy event on which you are pleased to congratulate and wellcome me to this City, demands all our gratitude; while the favourable sentiments you have thought proper to express of my conduct, intitles you to my warmest acknowledgements.

Disposed, at every suitable opportunity to acknowledge publicly our infinite obligations to the Supreme Ruler of the Universe for rescuing, our Country from the brink of destruction; I cannot fail at this time to ascribe all the honor of our late successes to the same glorious Being. And if my humble exertions have been made in any degree subservient to the execution of the divine purposes, a contemplation of the benediction of Heaven on our righteous Cause, the approbation of my virtuous Countrymen, & the testimony of my own Conscience, will be a sufficient reward and augment my felicity beyond anything which the world can bestow.

The establishment of Civil and Religious Liberty was the Motive which induced me to the Field—the object is attained—and it now remains to be my earnest wish & prayer, that the Citizens of the United States could make a wise and virtuous use of the blessings, placed before them; and that the reformed german Congregation in New York; may not only be conspicuous for their religious character, but as examplary, in support of our inestimable acquisitions, as their reverend Minister has been in the attainment of them.

(Papers, CCCCXCVI, 88-89.)

7

To the Ministers, Church Wardens, and Vestry-Men of the German Lutheran Congregation in and near Philadelphia.

GENTLEMEN: [April 20, 1789]

While I request you to accept my thanks for your kind address, I must profess myself highly gratified by the sentiments of esteem and consideration contained in it. The approbation my past conduct has received from so worthy a body of citizens, as that whose joy for my appointment you announce, is a proof of the indulgence with which my future transactions will be judged by them.

I could not, however, avoid apprehending that the partiality of my countrymen in favor of the measures now pursued has led them to expect too much from the present government; did not the same providence which has been visible in every stage of our progress to this interesting crisis, from a combination of circumstances, give us cause to hope for the accomplishment of all our reasonable desires.

Thus partaking with you in the pleasing anticipation of the blessings of a wise and efficient government; I flatter myself opportunities will not be wanting for me to shew my disposition to encourage the domestic and public virtues of industry, oeconomy, patriotism, philanthropy, and that righteousness which exalteth a nation.

I rejoice in having so suitable an occasion to testify the reciprocity of my esteem for the numerous people whom you represent. From the excellent character for diligence, sobriety, and virtue, which the Germans in general, who are settled in America, have ever maintained; I cannot forbear felicitating myself on receiving from so respectable a number of them such strong assurances of their affection for my person, confidence in my integrity, and zeal to support me in my endeavors for promoting the welfare of our common country.

So long as my conduct shall merit the approbation of the *wise and the good,* I hope to hold the same place in your affections, which your friendly declarations induce me to believe I possess at present; and amidst all the vicissitudes that may await me in this mutable state of existence, I shall earnestly desire the continuation of an interest in your intercessions at the Throne of Grace.

G. WASHINGTON

(Papers, CCCXXXIV, 24.)

8

To the General Committee, representing the United Baptist Churches in Virginia.

GENTLEMEN, [May, 1789]

I request that you will accept my best acknowledgments for your congratulation on my appointment to the first office in the nation. The kind manner in which you mention my past conduct equally claims the expression of my gratitude.

After we had, by the smiles of Heaven on our exertions, obtained the object for which we contended, I retired at the conclusion of the war, with an idea that my country could have no farther occasion for my services, and with the intention of never entering again into public life: But when the exigence of my country seemed to require me once more to engage in public affairs, an honest conviction of duty superseded my former resolution, and became my apology for deviating from the happy plan which I had adopted.

If I could have entertained the slightest apprehension that the Constitution framed in the Convention, where I had the honor to preside, might possibly endanger the religious rights of any ecclesiastical Society, certainly I would never have placed my signature to it; and if I could now conceive that the general Government might ever be so administered as to render the liberty of conscience insecure, I beg you will be persuaded that no one would be more zealous than myself to establish effectual barriers against the horrors of spiritual tyranny, and every species of religious persecution—For you, doubtless, remember that I have often expressed my sentiments, that every man, conducting himself as a good citizen, and being accountable to God alone for his religious opinions, ought to be protected in worshipping the Deity according to the dictates of his own conscience.

While I recollect with satisfaction that the religious Society of which you are Members, have been, throughout America, uniformly, and almost unanimously, the firm friends to civil liberty, and the persevering Promoters of our glorious revolution; I cannot hesitate to believe that they will be the faithful Supporters of a free, yet efficient general Government. Under this pleasing expectation I rejoice to assure them that they may rely on my best wishes and endeavors to advance their prosperity.

In the meantime be assured, Gentlemen, that I entertain a proper sense of your fervent supplications to God for my temporal and eternal happiness.

G. WASHINGTON

(Papers, CCCXXXIV, 84.)

9

To the General Assembly of the Presbyterian Church in the United States of America.

[May, 1789]

GENTLEMEN,

I receive with great sensibility the testimonial, given by the General Assembly of the Presbyterian Church in the United States of America, of the lively and unfeigned pleasure experienced by them on my appointment to the first office in the nation.

Although it will be my endeavor to avoid being elated by the too favorable opinion which your kindness for me may have induced you to express of the importance of my former conduct, and the effect of my future services: yet, conscious of the disinterestedness of my motives, it is not necessary for me to conceal the satisfaction I have felt upon finding, that my compliance with the call of my country, and my dependence on the assistance of Heaven to support me in my arduous undertakings, have, so far as I can learn, met the universal approbation of my countrymen.

While I reiterate the profession of my dependence upon Heaven as the source of all public and private blessings; I shall observe that the general prevalence of piety, philanthropy, honesty, industry and oeconomy seems, in the ordinary course of human affairs, particularly necessary for advancing and confirming the happiness of our country. While all men within our territories are protected in worshipping the Deity according to the dictates of their consciences; it is rationally to be expected from them in return, that they will all be emulous of evincing the sincerity of their professions by the innocence of their lives, and the beneficence of their actions: For no man, who is profligate in his morals, or a bad member of the civil community, can possibly be a true Christian, or a credit to his own religious society.

I desire you to accept my acknowledgements for your laudable endeavors to render men sober, honest, and good citizens, and the obedient subjects of a lawful government; as well as for your prayers to Almighty God for his blessing on our common country and the humble instrument, which he has been pleased to make use of in the administration of it's government.

G. WASHINGTON

(Papers, CCCXXXIV, 28.)

10

To the Bishops of the Methodist Episcopal Church in the United States of America

[May 29, 1789]

GENTLEMEN,

I return to you individually, and (through you) to your Society collectively in the United States my thanks for the demonstrations of affection, and the expressions of joy, offered in their behalf, on my late appointment. It shall still be my endeavor to manifest, by overt acts, the purity of my inclinations for promoting the happiness of mankind, as well as the sincerity of my desires to contribute whatever may be in my power towards the preservation of the civil and religious liberties of the American People. In pursuing this line of conduct, I hope, by the assistance of divine providence, not altogether to disappoint the confidence which you have been pleased to repose in me.

It always affords me satisfaction, when I find a concurrence in sentiment and practice between all conscientious men in acknowledgments of homage to the great Governor of the Universe, and in professions of support to a just, civil government. After mentioning that I trust the people of every denomination, who demean themselves as good citizens, will have occasion to be convinced that I shall always strive to prove a faithful and impartial Patron of genuine, vital religion: I must assure you in particular that I take in the kindest part the promise you make of presenting your prayers at the Throne of Grace for me, and that I likewise implore the divine benedictions on yourselves and your religious community.

G. WASHINGTON

(Papers, CCCXXXIV, 26.)

11

To the Ministers and Elders of the German Reformed Congregations in the United States.

[June 11, 1789]

GENTLEMEN,

I am happy in concurring with you in the sentiments of gratitude and piety towards Almighty-God, which are expressed with such fervency of devotion in your address; and in believing, that I shall always find in you, and the German Reformed Congregations in the United States a conduct correspondent to such worthy and pious expressions.

At the same time, I return you my thanks for the manifestation of your firm purpose to support in your persons a government founded in justice and equity, and for the promise that it will be your constant study to impress the minds of the People entrusted to your care with a due sense of the necessity of uniting reverence to such a government and obedience to it's laws with the duties and exercises of Religion.

Be assured, Gentlemen, it is, by such conduct, very much in the power of the virtuous Members of the community to alleviate the burden of the important office which I have accepted; and to give me Occasion to rejoice, in this world, for having followed therein the dictates of my conscience.

Be pleased also to accept my acknowledgements for the interest you so kindly take in the prosperity of my person, family, and administration.

May your devotions before the Throne of Grace be prevalent in calling down the blessings of Heaven upon yourselves and your country.

G. Washington.

(Papers, CCCXXXIV, 30.)

12

To the Directors of the Society of the United Brethren [Moravian] for Propagating the Gospel among the Heathen.

[July 10, 1789]

Gentlemen,

I receive with satisfaction the congratulations of your Society and of the Brethren's Congregations in the United States of America—For you may be persuaded that the approbation and good wishes of such a peaceable and virtuous Community cannot be indifferent to me.

You will also be pleased to accept my thanks for the Treatise which you present; and be assured of my patronage in your laudable undertakings.

In proportion as the general Government of the United States shall acquire strength by duration, it is probable they may have it in their power to extend a salutary influence to the aborigines in the extremities of their territory. In the meantime, it will be a desireable thing for the protection of the Union to co-operate, as far as the circumstances may conveniently admit, with the disinterested endeavors of your Society to civilize and christianize the Savages of the Wilderness.

Under these impressions I pray Almighty God to have you always in his holy keeping.

G. WASHINGTON

(Papers, CCCXXXIV, 34.)

13

To the Bishops, Clergy, and Laity of the Protestant Episcopal Church in the States of New York, New Jersey, Pennsylvania, Delaware, Maryland, Virginia, and South Carolina, in general Convention assembled.

[August 19, 1789]

GENTLEMEN,

I sincerely thank you for your affectionate congratulations on my election to the chief Magistracy of the United States.

After having received from my fellow-citizens in general the most liberal treatment—after having found them disposed to contemplate in the most flattering point of view, the performance of my military services, and the manner of my retirement at the close of the war—I feel that I have a right to console myself in my present arduous undertakings, with a hope that they will still be inclined to put the most favorable construction on the motives which may influence me in my future public transactions. The satisfaction arising from the indulgent opinion entertained by the American People of my conduct, will, I trust, be some security for preventing me from doing anything, which might justly incur the forfeiture of that opinion—and the consideration that human happiness and moral duty are inseparably connected, will always continue to prompt me to promote the progress of the former, by inculcating the practice of the latter.

On this occasion it would ill become me to conceal the joy I have felt in perceiving the fraternal affection which appears to encrease every day among the friends of genuine religion—It affords edifying prospects indeed to see Christians of different denominations dwell together in more charity, and conduct themselves in respect to each other with a more christian-like spirit than ever they have done in any former age, or in any other Nation.

I receive with the greater satisfaction your congratulations, on the establishment of the new constitution of government; because I believe it's mild, yet efficient, operations will tend to remove every remaining apprehension of those with whose opinions it may not entirely coincide, as well as to confirm the hopes of it's numerous friends; and because the moderation, patriotism, and wisdom of the present federal Legislature, seem to promise the restoration of Order, and our ancient virtues; the extension of genuine religion, and the consequent advancement of our respectability abroad, and of our substantial happiness at home.

I request most reverend and respected Gentlemen that you will accept my cordial thanks for your devout supplications to the Supreme Ruler of the Universe in behalf of me—May you, and the People whom you represent be the happy subjects of the divine benedictions both here and hereafter.

G. WASHINGTON.

(Papers, CCCXXXIV, 42.)

14

To the Synod of the Reformed Dutch Church in North America

[October, 1789]

GENTLEMEN,

I receive with a grateful heart your pious and affectionate address, and with truth declare to you that no circumstance of my life has affected me more sensibly or produced more pleasing emotions than the friendly congratulations, and strong assurances of support which I have received from my fellow-citizens of all descriptions upon my election to the Presidency of these United States.

I fear, Gentlemen, your goodness has led you to form too exalted an opinion of my virtues and merits—If such talents as I possess have been called into action by great events, and these events have terminated happily for our country, the glory should be ascribed to the manifest inter-position of an over-ruling Providence. My military services have been abundantly recompensed by the flattering appro-bation of a grateful people; and, if a faithful discharge of my civil duties can ensure a like reward, I shall feel myself richly compensated for any personal sacrifice I may have made by engaging again in public life.

The Citizens of the United States of America have given as signal a proof of their wisdom and virtue in framing and adopting a constitution of government, without bloodshed or the intervention of force, as they, upon a former occa-sion, exhibited to the world of their valor, fortitude, and perseverance; and it must be a pleasing circumstance to every friend of good order and social happiness to find that our new government is gaining strength and respectability among the citizens of this country in proportion as it's operations are known, and its effects felt.

You, Gentlemen, act the part of pious Christians and good citizens by your prayers and exertions to preserve that harmony and good will towards men which must be the basis of every political establishment; and I readily join with you that 'while just government protects all in their religious rights, true religion affords to government its surest support.'

I am deeply impressed with your good wishes for my present and future happiness—and I beseech the Almighty to take you and yours under his special care.

G. WASHINGTON.

(Papers, CCCXXXIV, 50.)

15

To the Congregational Ministers of the City of New Haven

[October 17, 1789]

GENTLEMEN,

The kind congratulations contained in your address claim and receive my grateful and affectionate thanks—Respecting, as I do, the favorable opinions of men distinguished for science and piety, it would be false delicacy to disavow the satisfaction, which I derive from their approbation of my public services and private conduct.

Regarding that deportment, which consists with true religion, as the best security of temporal peace, and the sure means of attaining eternal felicity, it will be my earnest endeavor (as far as human frailty may resolve) to inculcate the belief and practice of opinions which lead to the consummation of those desireable objects.

The tender interest which you have taken in my personal

happiness, and the obliging manner in which you express yourselves on the restoration of my health are so forcibly impressed on my mind as to render language inadequate to the utterance of my feelings.

If it shall please the great Disposer of events to listen to the pious supplications which you have preferred in my behalf, I trust that the remainder of my days will evince the gratitude of a heart devoted to the advancement of those objects, which receive the approbation of Heaven, and promote the happiness of our fellow-men.

My best prayers are offered to the Throne of Grace for your happiness and that of the Congregations committed to your care.

G. WASHINGTON.

(Papers, CCCXXXIV, 56.)

16

To the Religious Society Called Quakers, at Their Yearly Meeting for Pennsylvania, New Jersey, Delaware, and the Western Part of Maryland and Virginia

October, 1789

GENTLEMEN,

I receive with pleasure your affectionate address, and thank you for the friendly sentiments and good wishes, which you express for the success of my administration and for my personal happiness.

We have reason to rejoice in the prospect, that the present national government, which, by the favor of Divine Providence, was formed by the common counsels and peaceably established with the common consent of the people, will prove a blessing to every denomination of them. To render it such, my best endeavours shall not be wanting.

Government being, among other purposes, instituted to protect the persons and consciences of men from oppression, it certainly is the duty of rulers, not only to abstain from it themselves, but, according to their stations, to prevent it in others.

The liberty enjoyed by the people of these States, of worshipping Almighty God agreeably to their consciences, is not only among the choicest of their blessings, but also of their rights. While men perform their social duties faithfully, they do all that society or the state can with propriety demand or expect; and remain responsible only to their Maker for the religion, or modes of faith, which they may prefer or profess.

Your principles and conduct are well known to me; and it is doing the people called Quakers no more than justice to say, that (except their declining to share with others the burthen of the common defence) there is no denomination among us, who are more exemplary and useful citizens.

I assure you very explicitly, that in my opinion the conscientious scruples of all men should be treated with great delicacy and tenderness; and it is my wish and desire, that the laws may always be as extensively accomodated to them, as a due regard to the protection and essential interests of the nation may justify and permit.

GEORGE WASHINGTON.

(Papers, CCCXXXIV, 52.)

17

To the Ministers and Ruling Elders delegated to represent the churches in Massachusetts and New Hampshire, which compose the First Presbytery of the Eastward.

GENTLEMEN: [October, 1789]

The affectionate welcome which you are pleased to give me to the eastern part of this Union, would leave me without excuse did I fail to acknowledge the sensibility it awakens, and to express the most sincere return that a grateful sense of your goodness can suggest. To be approved by the praiseworthy, is a wish as natural to becoming ambition as its consequence is flattering to self-love. I am, indeed, much indebted to the favorable sentiments which you entertain towards me, and it will be my study to deserve them.

The tribute of thanksgiving which you offer to the gracious Father of lights, for his inspiration of our public councils with wisdom and firmness to complete the national Constitution, is worthy of men who, devoted to the pious purposes of religion, desire their accomplishment by such means as advance the temporal happiness of mankind.

And here, I am persuaded, you will permit me to observe, that the path of true piety is so plain as to require but little political attention. To this consideration we ought to ascribe the absence of any regulation respecting religion from the Magna Charta of our country.

To the guidance of the ministers of the gospel this important object is, perhaps, more properly committed. It will be your care to instruct the ignorant, to reclaim the devious; and in the progress of morality and science, to which our government will give every furtherance, we may expect confidently, the advancement of true religion and the completion of happiness. I pray the munificent rewarder of every virtue, that your agency in this good work may receive its compensation here and hereafter.

GEORGE WASHINGTON.

(Papers, CCCXXXIV, 80.)

18

To the Members of the Religious Society of Free Quakers

[March, 1790]

GENTLEMEN,

I desire to assure you of the sensibility with which I receive your congratulations on my appointment to the highest office and most extended trust which can be confided by a free People—and I thank you with sincerity for the obliging terms in which you express yourselves in my behalf.

Ever happy in being favored with the approbation of my fellow-citizens, the time at which yours is declared does not diminish my sense of the obligation it confers.

Having always considered the conscientious scruples of religious belief as resting entirely with the sects that profess, or the individuals who entertain them, I cannot, consistent with this uniform sentiment, otherwise notice the circumstances referred to in your address, than by adding the tribute of my acknowledgement, to that of our country, for those services which the members of your particular community rendered to the common cause in the course of our revolution—And by assuring you that, as our present government was instituted with an express view to general happiness, it will be my earnest endeavor, in discharging the duties confided to me with faithful impartiality, to realise the hope of common protection which you expect from the measures of that government.

Impressed with gratitude for your supplications to the Supreme Being in my favor, I entreat his gracious beneficence in your behalf.

(Papers, CCCXXXIV, 116-17.)

19

To the Roman Catholics in the United States of America.

GENTLEMEN,   [March 15, 1790]

While I now receive with much satisfaction your congratulations on my being called, by a unanimous vote, to the first station in my country; I cannot but duly notice your politeness in offering an apology for the unavoidable delay. As that delay has given you an opportunity of realizing, instead of anticipating, the benefits of the general government, you will do me the justice to believe that your testimony of the encrease of the public prosperity enhances the pleasure which I should otherwise have experienced from your affectionate address.

I feel that my conduct in war and in peace has met with more general approbation than could reasonably have been expected: and I find myself disposed to consider that fortunate circumstance, in a great degree, resulting from the able support, and extraordinary candor of my fellow-citizens of all denominations.

The prospect of national prosperity now before us is truly animating, and ought to excite the exertions of all good men to establish and secure the happiness of their country, in the permanent duration of its freedom and independence. America, under the smiles of a divine Providence—the protection of a good government—the cultivation of manners, morals, and piety—can hardly fail of attaining an uncommon degree of eminence in literature, commerce, agriculture—improvements at home, and respectability abroad.

As mankind become more liberal, they will be more apt to allow, that all those who conduct themselves as worthy members of the community, are equally entitled to the protection of civil government. I hope ever to see America among the foremost nations in examples of justice and liberality. And I presume that your fellow-citizens will not forget the patriotic part which you took in the accomplishment of their revolution, and the establishment of their government; or the important assistance which they received from a nation in which the Roman Catholic religion is professed.

I thank you, Gentlemen, for your kind concern for me. While my life and my health shall continue, in whatever situation I may be, it shall be my constant endeavor to justify the favorable sentiments you are pleased to express of my conduct.—And may the members of your Society in America, animated alone by the pure spirit of Christianity, and still conducting themselves as the faithful subjects of our free government, enjoy every temporal and spiritual felicity.

(Papers, CCCXXXIV, 100.)

G. WASHINGTON.

20

To the Hebrew-Congregation of the City of Savannah

GENTLEMEN,   [May, 1790]

I thank you with great sincerity for your congratulations on my appointment to the office, which I have the honor to hold by the unanimous choice of my fellow-citizens: and especially for the expressions which you are pleased to use in testifying the confidence that is reposed in me by your congregation.

As the delay which has naturally intervened between my election and your address has afforded an opportunity for appreciating the merits of the federal-government, and for communicating your sentiments of its administration—I have rather to express my satisfaction than regret at a circumstance, which demonstrates (upon experiment) your attachment to the former as well as approbation of the latter.

I rejoice that a spirit of liberality and philanthropy is much more prevalent than it formerly was among the enlightened nations of the earth; and that your brethren will benefit thereby in proportion as it shall become still more extensive. Happily the people of the United States have, in many instances, exhibited examples worthy of imitation—The salutary influence of which will doubtless extend much farther, if gratefully enjoying those blessings of peace which (under favor of Heaven) have been obtained by fortitude in war, they shall conduct themselves with reverence to the Deity, and charity towards their fellow-creatures.

May the same wonder-working Deity, who long since delivering the Hebrews from their Egyptian oppressors planted them in the promised land—whose providential agency has lately been conspicuous in establishing these United States as an independent nation—still continue to water them with the dews of Heaven and to make the inhabitants of every denomination participate in the temporal and spiritual blessings of that people whose God is Jehovah.

G. WASHINGTON.

(Papers, CCCXXXIV, 131-32.)

21

To the Hebrew Congregation in New Port, Rhode Island

GENTLEMEN,   [August 17, 1790]

While I receive with much satisfaction your address replete with expressions of affection and esteem, I rejoice in the opportunity of assuring you that I shall always retain a grateful remembrance of the cordial welcome I experienced in my visit to NewPort from all classes of Citizens.

The reflection on the days of difficulty and danger which are past is rendered the more sweet from a consciousness that they are succeeded by days of uncommon prosperity and security. If we have the wisdom to make the best use of the advantages with which we are now favored, we cannot fail, under the just administration of a good government to become a great and happy people.

The Citizens of the United States of America have a right to applaud themselves for having given to Mankind examples of an enlarged and liberal policy, a policy worthy of imitation. All possess alike liberty of conscience and immunities of citizenship. It is now no more that toleration is spoken of, as if it was by the indulgence of one class of people, that another enjoyed the exercise of their inherent natural rights. For happily the Government of the United States, which gives to bigotry no sanction, to persecution no assistance, requires only that they who live under its protection should demean themselves as good citizens, in giving it on all occasions their effectual support.

It would be inconsistent with the frankness of my character not to avow that I am pleased with your favorable opinion of my administration, and fervent wishes for my felicity.

May the children of the Stock of Abraham, who dwell in this land, continue to merit and enjoy the good will of the other inhabitants, while every one shall sit in safety under his own vine and fig tree, and there shall be none to make him afraid.

May the Father of all mercies scatter light and not darkness in our paths, and make us all in our several vocations useful here, and in his own due time and way everlastingly happy.

G. WASHINGTON.

(Papers, CCCXXXV, 19-20.)

22

To the Clergy of the Town of Newport in the State of Rhode-Island.

[August 17, 1790]

GENTLEMEN,

The salutations of the Clergy of the Town of Newport on my arrival in the State of Rhode Island are rendered the more acceptable on account of the liberal sentiments and just ideas which they are known to entertain respecting civil and religious liberty.

I am inexpressibly happy that by the smiles of divine Providence, my weak but honest endeavors to serve my country have hitherto been crowned with so much success, and apparently given such satisfaction to those in whose cause they were exerted. The same benignant influence, together with the concurrent support of all real friends to their country will still be necessary to enable me to be in any degree useful to this numerous and free People over whom I am called to preside.

Wherefore I return you, Gentlemen, my hearty thanks for your solemn invocation of Almighty God that every temporal and spiritual blessing may be dispensed to me, and that, under my administration the families of these States may enjoy peace and prosperity, with all the blessings attendant on civil and religious liberty—In the participation of which blessings may you have an ample share.

G. WASHINGTON.

(Papers, CCCXXXIV, 149-50.)

23

To the Convention of the Universal Church lately assembled in Philadelphia

[Summer, 1790]

GENTLEMEN,

I thank you cordially for the congratulations which you offer on my appointment to the office I have the honor to hold in the government of the United States.

It gives me the most sensible pleasure to find, that, in our nation, however different are the sentiments of citizens on religious doctrines, they generally concur in one thing, for their political professions and practices are almost universally friendly to the order and happiness of our civil institutions—I am also happy in finding this disposition particularly evinced by your Society. It is moreover my earnest desire, that the members of every association or community, throughout the United States, may make such use of the auspicious years of Peace, liberty, and free enquiry, with which they are now favored, as they shall hereafter find occasion to rejoice for having done.

With great satisfaction I embrace this opportunity to express my acknowledgements for the interest my affectionate fellow-citizens have taken in my recovery from a late dangerous indisposition, and I assure you, Gentlemen, that in mentioning my obligations for the effusions of your benevolent wishes on my behalf, I feel animated with new zeal, that my conduct may ever be worthy of your favorable opinion, as well as such as shall in every respect best comport with the character of an intelligent and accountable being.

G. WASHINGTON

(Papers, CCCXXXV, 15-16.)

24

To the Hebrew Congregations in the Cities of Philadelphia, New York, Charleston and Richmond.

[December 13, 1790]

GENTLEMEN,

The liberal sentiment towards each other which marks every political and religious denomination of men in this country stands unrivalled in the history of nations—The affection of such a people is a treasure beyond the reach of calculation; and the repeated proofs which my fellow citizens have given of their attachment to me, and approbation of my doings form the purest source of my temporal felicity—The affectionate expressions of your address again excite my gratitude, and receive my warmest acknowledgements.

The power and goodness of the Almighty were strongly manifested in the events of our late glorious revolution.—and his kind interposition in our behalf has been no less visible in the establishment of our present equal government—In war he directed the sword—and in peace he has ruled in our councils—my agency in both has been guided by the best intentions, and a sense of the duty which I owe my country: and as my exertions hitherto have been amply rewarded by the approbation of my fellow-citizens, I shall endeavor to deserve a continuance of it by my future conduct.

May the same temporal and eternal blessings which you implore for me, rest upon your congregations.

G. WASHINGTON.

(Papers, CCCXXXV, 32-33.)

25

To the Congregational Church and Society at Midway (formerly St. John's Parish) State of Georgia

[May, 1791]

GENTLEMEN,

I learn with gratitude proportioned to the occasion your attachment to my person, and the pleasure you express on my election to the Presidency of the United States.

Your sentiments on the happy influence of our equal government impress me with the most sensible satisfaction—they vindicate the great interests of humanity—they reflect honor on the liberal minds that entertain them—and they promise the continuance and improvement of that tranquillity, which is essential to the welfare of nations, and the happiness of men.

You over-rate my best exertions when you ascribe to them the blessings which our country so eminently enjoys.—From the gallantry and fortitude of her citizens, under the auspices of heaven, America has derived her independence—To their industry and the natural advantages of the country she is indebted for her prosperous situation—From their virtue she may expect long to share the protection of a free and equal government, which their wisdom has established, and which experience justifies, as admirably adapted to our social wants and individual felicity.

Continue, my fellow-citizens, to cultivate the peace and

harmony which now subsist between you, and your indian neighbours—the happy consequence is immediate, the reflection, which arises on justice and benevolence, will be everlastingly grateful. A knowledge of your happiness will lighten the cares of my station, and be among the most pleasing of their rewards.

G. WASHINGTON.

(Papers, CCCXXXV, 81.)

26

To the United Brethren in Wachovia [Georgia]

[May, 1791]

GENTLEMEN,

I am greatly indebted to your respectful and affectionate expressions of personal regard, and I am not less obliged by the patriotic sentiments contained in your address.

From a Society, whose governing principles are industry and love of order, much may be expected towards the improvement and prosperity of the country in which their Settlements are formed, and experience authorizes the belief that much will be obtained.

Thanking you with grateful sincerity for your prayers in my behalf I desire to assure you of my best wishes for your social and individual happiness.

G. WASHINGTON.

(Papers, CCCXXXV, 95.)

27

To the Members of the New Church at Baltimore

[Jan. 27, 1793]

GENTLEMEN,

It has ever been my pride to merit the approbation of my

fellow citizens by a faithful & honest discharge of the duties annexed to those stations in which they have been pleased to place me; and the dearest rewards of my services have been those testimonies of esteem & confidence with which they have honored me. But to the manifest interposition of an over-ruling Providence, & to the patriotic exertions of United America are to be ascribed those events which have given us a respectable rank among the nations of the Earth.

We have abundant reason to rejoice that in this Land the light of truth & reason has triumphed over the power of bigotry and superstition, and that every person may here worship God according to the dictates of his own heart. In this enlightened age & in this Land of equal liberty it is our boast, that a man's religious tenets will not forfeit the protection of the Laws, nor deprive him of the right of attaining & holding the highest offices that are known in the United States.

Your prayers for my present & future felicity are received with gratitude; and I sincerely wish, Gentlemen, that you may in your social & individual capacities taste those blessings which a gracious God bestows upon the Righteous.

G. WASHINGTON

(Papers, CCCXXXV, 110.)

28

To the Rector, Church Wardens & Vestrymen of the United Episcopal Churches of Christ and St. Peters.

[March 2, 1797]

GENTLEMEN,

To this public testimony of your approbation of my conduct and affection for my person I am not insensible,—and your prayers for my present and future happiness merit my warmest acknowledgments. It is with peculiar satisfaction I can say, that, prompted by a high sense of duty in my attendance on public worship, I have been gratified, during my residence among you, by the liberal and interesting discourses which have been delivered in your Churches.

Believing that that Government alone can be approved by Heaven, which promotes peace and secures protection to its Citizens in every thing that is dear and interesting to them, it has been the great object of my administration to insure those invaluable ends; and when, to a consciousness of the purity of intentions, is added the approbation of my fellow Citizens, I shall experience in my retirement that heartfelt satisfaction which can only be exceeded by the hope of future happiness.

G. WASHINGTON

(Papers, CCCXXXVI, 279.)

29

To the Clergy of different denominations residing in and near the city of Philadelphia.

[March 3, 1797]

GENTLEMEN,

Not to acknowledge with gratitude and sensibility the affectionate addresses and benevolent wishes of my fellow citizens, on my retiring from publick life, would prove that I have been unworthy of the confidence which they have been pleased to repose in me.

And among those publick testimonies of attachment and approbation, none can be more grateful than that of so respectable a body as yours.

Believing, as I do, that *Religion and Morality are the*

essential pillars of civil society; I view with unspeakable pleasure, that harmony and brotherly love which characterize the Clergy of different denominations, as well in this, as in other parts of the United States; exhibiting to the world a new and interesting spectacle, at once the pride of our country and the surest basis of universal harmony.

That your labours for the good of mankind may be crowned with success; that your temporal enjoyments may be commensurate with your merits: and that the future reward of good and faithful servants may be yours, I shall not cease to supplicate the Divine Author of life and felicity.

G. WASHINGTON

(Papers, CCCXXXVI, 280-81.)

NOTES

NOTE: The abbreviation *G.W.* in these notes refers to John C. Fitzpatrick, ed., *The Writings of George Washington* (39 vols.; Washington, D.C., 1931-44). *Papers* refers to the unpublished Papers of George Washington, in the Library of Congress.

CHAPTER I

1. Edward C. McGuire, *The Religious Opinions and Character of Washington* (New York, 1836), pp. 162-67. McGuire's source was a "respectable literary journal" published in New York (p. 162). Apparently the anecdote first appeared in the *New York Mirror* in May, 1834. See John F. Watson, *Annals and Occurrences of New York City and State* (Philadelphia, 1846), pp. 304-5.

2. William J. Johnstone, *How Washington Prayed* (New York, 1932), p. 28.

3. B.F. Morris, *Christian Life and Character of the Civil Institutions of the United States* (Philadelphia, 1864), p. 166.

4. Philip Slaughter, *Christianity the Key to the Character and Career of Washington: A Discourse Delivered before the Ladies of the Mt. Vernon Association of the Union, at Pohick Church, Truro Parish, Virginia, on the Thirtieth Day of May, 1886* (Washington, D.C., 1886), p. 2.

5. Morris, *op. cit.,* p. 11.

6. William Meade, *Old Churches, Ministers and Families of Virginia* (2 vols.; Philadelphia, 1857), II, 243.

7. J. V. Nash, "The Religion and Philosophy of Washington," *Open Court,* XLIII (February, 1932), 73.

8. M.L. Weems, *The Life of George Washington* (29th ed.; Frankford near Philadelphia, 1826); McGuire, *op. cit.;* Meade, *op. cit.;* William J. Johnstone, *George Washington the Christian* (Cincinnati, 1919); Joseph Buffington, *The Soul of Washington* (Philadelphia, 1936); W. Herbert Burk, *Washington's Prayers* (Norristown, Pennsylvania, 1907).

9. McGuire, *op. cit.,* pp. 168, 400; Morris, *op. cit.,* p. 501.

10. Burk, *op. cit.;* Rupert Hughes, *George Washington the Human Being and the Hero, 1732-1762* (New York, 1926), Appendix II, "The Spurious Prayers," pp. 552-59.

11. Johnstone, *How Washington Prayed,* p. 34; John F. Watson, *Annals of Philadelphia and Pennsylvania, in the Olden Time* (3 vols.; Philadelphia, 1881), I, 422.

12. Johnstone, *How Washington Prayed,* p. 34.

13. Albert R. Beatty, "Was Washington Religious?" *National Republic,* XX (March, 1933), 18.

14. Samuel Greene Arnold, *The Life of George Washington* (New York, 1840), p. 117.

15. Johnstone, *How Washington Prayed,* p. 70.

16. Woodrow Wilson, *George Washington* (New York, 1896), p. 227.

17. C.M. Kirkland, *Memoirs of Washington* (New York, 1857), pp. **478-79.**

18. Morris, *op. cit.*, p. 502.

19. T.W.J. Wylie, *Washington, a Christian: A Discourse Preached February 23, 1862, in the First Reformed Presbyterian Church, Philadelphia* (Philadelphia, 1862), p. 28.

20. Watson, *Annals of New York*, p. 305.

21. Rupert Hughes, *George Washington, the Savior of the States, 1777-1781* (New York, 1930), p. 282.

22. Harold Kellock, *Parson Weems of the Cherry Tree* (New York, 1928), p. 86.

23. Weems, *op. cit.*, p. 184.

24. Watson, *Annals of Philadelphia*, I, 580.

25. Weems, *op. cit.*, called her Sarah (p. 184); Wylie, *op. cit.*, called her Betty (p. 29n.); Morris, *op. cit.*, called her Martha (p. 298).

26. Morris, *op. cit.*, p. 298.

27. John C. Fitzpatrick, *The Spirit of the Revolution* (Boston and New York, 1924), pp. 88-89; Hughes, *Washington, Savior of the States,* pp. 270-77; Samuel Eliot Morison, *The Young Man Washington* (Cambridge, 1932), p. 38.

28. Buffington, *op. cit.*, p. 119.

29. Hughes, *Washington, Savior of the States*, p. 280.

30. Morris, *op. cit.*, p. 297.

31. W. Herbert Burk, *The Washington Window in the Washington Memorial Chapel, Valley Forge* (Norristown, Pennsylvania, 1926); J. Leroy Miller, "Where Washington Prayed Thousands Now Will Pray," *American Magazine*, CVIII (August, 1929).

32. Hughes, *Washington, Savior of the States*, p. 280.

33. *William and Mary Quarterly*, Third Series, XII (1955), 477-78; *Time*, LXV (April 4, 1955), 65.

34. David Hosack, *Memoir of DeWitt Clinton* (New York, 1829), pp. 183-84n.

35. McGuire, *op. cit.*, p. 412.

36. *Ibid.*, p. 414.

37. *Ibid.*, p. 413.

38. Edward Slater Dunlap, *George Washington as a Christian and Churchman* (Washington, D.C., 1932), p. 8; McGuire, *op. cit.*, p. 412.

39. "Washington at the Communion Table in Morristown, New Jersey," *Presbyterian Magazine*, I (December, 1851), 569; "Washington at Morristown during the Winter of 1779-80," *Harper's New Monthly Magazine*, XVIII (February, 1859), 295; Johnstone, *Washington the Christian*, p. 89.

40. James M. Buckley, "Washington as a Christian and a Communicant," *Independent*, L (February 24, 1898), 241.

41. E.S. Dunlap, "Washington as a Christian," *New York Daily Tribune*, May 26, 1902.

42. "Washington at Morristown," *Harper's*, XVIII, 293.

43. "Washington as a Christian," *Independent*, L, 241.

44. "Washington at Morristown," *Harper's*, XVIII, 295.

45. "Washington at the Communion Table," *Presbyterian Magazine*, I, 570.

46. *Albany Daily Advertiser,* Saturday, October 29, 1831. See also *Discussion on the Existence of God and the Authenticity of the Bible, between Origen Bacheler and Robert Dale Owen* (2 vols.; London, 1840), II, 231.

47. Frances Wright, *Course of Popular Lectures* (New York, 1831), pp. 10-11, quoted in Herbert Morais, *Deism in Eighteenth Century America* (London, 1934), p. 113.

48. *Discussion between Bacheler and Owen.*

49. *Ibid.,* II, 122.

50. *Ibid.,* II, 140.

51. *Ibid.,* II, 231-32.

52. *Ibid,* II, 233.

53. *Ibid.,* II, 234.

54. *Ibid.,* II, 235.

55. William L. Stone, "Was Washington a Christian," *Magazine of American History,* XIII (June, 1885), 597.

56. McGuire, *op. cit.,* p. v.

57. *Ibid.,* p. 73.

58. *Ibid.,* p. 75.

59. *New-York Review and Quarterly Church Journal,* I (March, 1837), 236.

60. *Ibid.,* p. 237.

61. Meade, *Old Churches* (1857); Morris, *Christian Life and Character* (1864); Slaughter, *Christianity the Key to Washington* (1886); Eliphalet Nott Potter, *Washington, A Model in His Library and Life* (New York, 1895); Burk, *Washington's Prayers* (1907); Johnstone, *Washington the Christian* (1919); Burk, *Washington Window* (1926); Buffington, *Soul of Washington* (1936).

62. McGuire, *op. cit.,* pp. 47-67.

63. "Washington as a Christian," *Independent,* L, 206; Joseph Buffington, *An Overlooked Side of Washington: Being the Bi-Centennial Address Made on Washington's Birthday, 1932, at Valley Forge Memorial Chapel* (Philadelphia, 1932), p. 31.

64. Albert R. Beatty, "Washington's Christmases," *National Republic,* XX (January, 1933), 3.

65. Buffington, *Overlooked Side of Washington;* Buffington, *Soul of Washington.*

66. Buffington, *Soul of Washington,* p. 47.

67. *Ibid.,* p. 55.

68. *Ibid.,* p. 47.

69. Buffington, *Overlooked Side of Washington,* p. 8; Jared Sparks, ed., *The Writings of George Washington* (12 vols.; Boston, 1837), XII, 399.

70. Buffington, *Overlooked Side of Washington,* pp. 8-9.

71. Buffington, *Soul of Washington,* pp. 53-54.

72. *Ibid.,* pp. 54-55.

73. *Ibid.,* p. 105.

74. *Ibid.,* p. 110.

75. McGuire, *op. cit.,* p. 76.

76. Weems, *op. cit.*, p. 188.

77. Rev. Frank Landon Humphreys, *George Washington, the Church-man* (n.p., 1932), p. 13.

CHAPTER II

1. Thomas O'Gorman, *A History of the Roman Catholic Church in the United States* (New York, 1916), p. 289.

2. William Cathcart, *The Baptists and the American Revolution* (Philadelphia, 1876), p. 42.

3. Ben M. Bogard, *President Washington a Baptist* (Little Rock, Arkansas, 1921?), pp. 10-12. See also L. C. Barnes, "The John Gano Evidence of George Washington's Religion," *Bulletin of William Jewell College,* Series No. 24, No. 1 (September 15, 1926).

4. Marguerite Beck Block, *The New Church in the New World* (New York, 1932), p. 411.

5. Richard Eddy, *Universalism in America: A History* (2 vols.; Boston, 1886), I, 332.

6. Lars P. Qualben, *The Lutheran Church in Colonial America* (New York, 1940), p. 269.

7. A.B. Faust, *The German Element in the United States* (2 vols.; Boston and New York, 1909), I, 301.

8. J.I. Good, *History of the German Reformed Church in the United States, 1725-1792* (Reading, Pennsylvania, 1899), p. 617.

9. J.B. Wakeley, *Anecdotes of the Wesleys: Illustrative of their Character and Personal History* (New York, 1870), pp. 119-20.

10. W.P. Strickland, *The Pioneer Bishop: or, the Life and Times of Francis Asbury* (New York, 1858), p. 231. Asbury met Washington personally only once. On May 26, 1785, he and Thomas Coke visited Mount Vernon and discussed slavery with Washington. *The Journals of the Rev. Francis Asbury . . . from August 7, 1771, to December 7, 1815* (3 vols.; New York, 1821), I, 496.

11. Harry Simonhoff, *Jewish Notables in America, 1776-1865* (New York, 1956), p. 51.

12. Isaac Markens, *The Hebrews in America* (New York, 1888), p. 83.

13. Peter Wiernik, *History of the Jews in America* (New York, 1931), p. 100.

14. Charles H. Callahan, *Washington the Man and the Mason* (Washington, D.C., 1913), p. 95.

15. Philip A. Bruce, *Institutional History of Virginia in the Seventeenth Century* (2 vols.; New York, 1910), I, 62-93.

16. Washington to Daniel McCarty, Mount Vernon, February 22, 1784, *G.W.*, XXVII, 341-42.

17. Paul Wilstach, *Mount Vernon, Washington's Home and the Nation's Shrine* (Garden City, 1916), p. 106; Jared Sparks, ed., *The Writings of George Washington* (12 vols.; Boston, 1837), XII, 400.

18. Philip Slaughter, *The History of Truro Parish in Virginia* (Philadelphia, 1908), pp. 34 ff.

19. David John Mays, *Edmund Pendleton, 1721-1803* (2 vols.; Cambridge, 1952), II, 133-37.

20. Slaughter, *Truro Parish*, p. 97.

21. M.L. Weems, *The Life of George Washington* (29th ed.; Frankford near Philadelphia, 1826), pp. 197-98.

22. Paul Leicester Ford, *The True George Washington* (Philadelphia, 1896), p. 78.

23. *Memoirs of Washington, by His Adopted Son, George Washington Parke Custis, with a Memoir of the Author, by his Daughter; and Illustrative and Explanatory Notes by Benson J. Lossing* (New York, 1859), p. 173.

24. Ford, *op. cit.*, p. 78. See John C. Fitzpatrick, ed., *The Diaries of George Washington* (4 vols.; Boston, 1925), I, 107-64; 245-304.

25. Ford, *op. cit.*, p. 79. For typical entries regarding his activities on Sunday, see *Diaries*, I, 113, 116, 156, 247, 254.

26. *Diaries*, I, 246, 247, 252, 253, 257, 265, 276, 277.

27. Washington to Burwell Bassett, Mount Vernon, August 28, 1762, *G.W.*, XXXVII, 484-85.

28. John C. Fitzpatrick, *George Washington Himself* (Indianapolis, 1933), pp. 130-31. See also *Washington as a Religious Man*, Pamphlet Number 5 of the Series "Honor to George Washington," ed. Dr. Albert Bushnell Hart (Washington, D.C.: George Washington Bicentennial Commission, 1931), pp. 3-5.

29. To the Secretary of War (Private), Mount Vernon, April 23, 1799, *G.W.*, XXXVII, 187-88.

30. Fitzpatrick, *op. cit.*, p. 130.

31. *Diaries*, IV, 50.

32. *Ibid.*, IV, 203.

33. *Ibid.*, IV, 212.

34. *Ibid.*, I, 265; II, 119; IV, 54.

35. Papers, CCCXXXVI, 278-79.

36. Bird Wilson, *Memoir of the Life of the Right Reverend William White* (Philadelphia, 1839), p. 190.

37. *Diaries*, II, 153.

38. Edward C. McGuire, *The Religious Opinions and Character of Washington* (New York, 1836), p. 143.

39. Joseph Buffington, *The Soul of Washington* (Philadelphia, 1936), p. 95.

40. Eleanor Parke Custis to Jared Sparks, February 26, 1833, in Sparks, ed., *Writings of Washington*, XII, 406.

41. William White to Rev. B.C.C. Parker, Philadelphia, November 28, 1832, in Bird Wilson, *Memoir of White*, p. 189. See also Sparks, ed., *Writings of Washington*, XII, 408.

42. Sparks, *op. cit.*, XII, 406.

43. *Ibid.*, p. 406.

44. William White to Colonel Hugh Mercer, Philadelphia, August

15, 1835, in Wilson, *Memoir of . . . the Right Reverend William White*, p. 197.

45. Dr. James Abercrombie to Origen Bacheler, November 29, 1831, *Magazine of American History*, XIII (June, 1885), 597.

46. See above, p. 16.

47. For some of these stories, see William Meade, *Old Churches, Ministers and Families of Virginia* (2 vols.; Philadelphia, 1857), II, 491-95; "Washington as a Communicant of the Church, Testimony of an Eye-Witness to Washington's Frequent Communions while President," *Churchman* (New York), LXXIX (June 3, 1899), 795-98.

48. Edward Slater Dunlap, *George Washington as a Christian and Churchman* (Washington, D.C., 1932), p. 10.

49. *The Journal of Claude Blanchard, Commissary of the French Auxiliary Army Sent to the United States during the American Revolution, 1780-1783*, trans. William Duane, ed. Thomas Balch (Albany, New York, 1876), p. 118.

50. Rufus W. Griswold, *The Republican Court* (New York, 1855), p. 164.

51. Ashbel Green, *The Life of Ashbel Green* (New York, 1849), p. 267.

52. William Harden, "William McWhir, an Irish Friend of Washington," *Georgia Historical Quarterly*, I (September, 1917), 197-218.

53. William B. Sprague, *Annals of the American Pulpit* (9 vols.; New York, 1859-69), III, 440.

54. *Magazine of American History*, XXI (June, 1889), 518.

55. *Proceedings of the American Antiquarian Society at the Semi-Annual Meeting, April 30, 1879, at the Hall of the American Academy of Arts and Sciences, Boston* (Worcester, Massachusetts, 1880), LXXIII-LXXV (1879-80), 75.

56. Katharine McCook Knox, *The Sharples, Their Portraits of George Washington and His Contemporaries* (New Haven, 1930), pp. 13, 64-65.

57. James Walter, *Memorials of Washington and of Mary, His Mother, and Martha, His Wife, from Letters and Papers of Robert Clary and James Sharples* (New York, 1887).

58. *Ibid.*, p. 233.

59. *Massachusetts Historical Society Proceedings*, 2d. Series, III (Boston, 1886-87), 179-89.

60. McGuire, *op. cit.*, p. 404.

61. Eliphalet Nott Potter, *Washington, A Model in His Library and Life* (New York, 1895), p. 181.

62. Washington to Rev. John Rodgers, Headquarters, June 11, 1783, *G.W.*, XXVII, 1.

63. P. Marion Simms, *The Bible in America* (New York, 1936), p. 132.

64. Washington to Rev. Clement Cruttwell, Philadelphia, July 10, 1795, *G.W.*, XXXIV, 234.

65. Washington's Last Will and Testament, July 9, 1799, *G.W.*, XXXVII, 286.

66. Washington to Charles Thomson, Philadelphia, March 5, 1795, *G.W.*, XXX, 286.

67. See, for example, Washington to John Augustine Washington,

White Plains, November 6, 1776, *G.W.*, VI, 247; Washington to Landon Carter, October 17, 1796, *G.W.*, XXXV, 246.

68. *G.W.*, XXX, 301-2.

69. Washington to Burwell Bassett, Mount Vernon, August 28, 1762, *G.W.*, XXXVII, 485.

70. Washington to Rev. Jonathan Boucher, Mount Vernon, May 21, 1772, *G.W.*, III, 84.

71. Washington to Mrs. Annis Boudinot Stockton, Rocky Hill, September 2, 1783, *G.W.*, XXVII, 127-29.

72. McGuire, *op. cit.*, p. 404. Robert C. Hartnett, S.J., of Fordham University, noted with satisfaction that the first part of Washington's letter showed him to have been "on speaking terms with 'Romish' practices," in F. Ernest Johnson, ed., *Wellsprings of the American Spirit* (New York, 1948), p. 53.

CHAPTER III

1. A.J. Russell, *Their Religion* (New York, 1935), p. 223.

2. To the General Assembly of the Presbyterian Church in the United States of America [May, 1789], Papers, CCCXXXIV, 28.

3. *G.W.*, XXXV, 229-30.

4. *Discussion on the Existence of God and the Authenticity of the Bible, between Origen Bacheler and Robert Dale Owen* (2 vols.; London, 1840), II, 99.

5. Edward C. McGuire, *The Religious Opinions and Character of Washington* (New York, 1836), p. 75.

6. *Ibid.*, p. 77.

7. *Ibid.*, p. 78.

8. Victor Hugo Paltsits, *Washington's Farewell Address* (New York, 1935), pp. xiv-xv.

9. Washington to Robert Dinwiddie, June 12, 1757, *G.W.*, II, 56.

10. Washington to Dinwiddie, Mount Vernon, September 23, 1756, *G.W.*, I, 470.

11. Washington to John Blair, Fort Loudoun, April 17, 1758, *G.W.*, II, 178.

12. Orders, Fort Cumberland, September 19, 1755 and July 7, 1756, *G.W.*, I, 179, 396.

13. Orders, Winchester, September 25, 1756, *G.W.*, I, 473.

14. Washington to Colonel George Baylor, Morristown, May 23, 1777, *G.W.*, VIII, 109.

15. J.T. Headley, *The Chaplains and Clergy of the Revolution* (New York, 1864), pp. 60-61.

16. Washington to Governor Jonathan Trumbull, Cambridge, December 15, 1775, *G.W.*, IV, 164.

17. Worthington Chauncey Ford, ed., *Journals of the Continental Congress* (34 vols.; Washington, D.C., 1904-37), II, 220.

18. Washington to the President of Congress, Cambridge, December 31, 1775, *G.W.*, IV, 197-98.

19. General Orders, Cambridge, February 7, 1776, *G.W.*, IV, 307.

20. Washington to the President of Congress, New York, June 18, 1776, *G.W.*, V, 192-93.

21. General Orders, Headquarters, New York, July 9, 1776, *G.W.*, V, 244-45.

22. Resolution of April 11, 1777, *Journals of Continental Congress*, VII, 256; resolution of May 27, 1777, *ibid.*, VIII, 390.

23. Washington to the President of Congress, Middle Brook, June 8, 1777, *G.W.*, VIII, 203-4.

24. General Orders, Cambridge, July 4, 1775, *G.W.*, III, 309.

25. General Orders, Headquarters, Middle Brook, June 28, 1777, *G.W.*, VIII, 308.

26. General Orders, Saturday, March 22, 1783, *G.W.*, XXVI, 250.

27. General Orders, Headquarters, Cambridge, July 4, 1775, *G.W.*, III, 309.

28. General Orders, Headquarters, New York, May 15, 1776, *G.W.*, V, 43.

29. General Orders, Headquarters, at the Gulph, December 17, 1777, *G.W.*, X, 168.

30. General Orders, Headquarters, at Wentz's, Worcester Township, October 18, 1777, *G.W.*, IX, 391.

31. General Orders, Headquarters, Valley Forge, May 5, 1778, *G.W.*, XI, 354.

32. General Orders, October 20, 1781, *G.W.*, XXIII, 247.

33. General Orders, Headquarters, Cambridge, February 27, 1776, *G.W.*, IV, 355.

34. General Orders, Headquarters, New York, August 12, 1776, *G.W.*, V, 423.

35. General Orders, Headquarters, New York, August 3, 1776, *G.W.*, V, 367.

36. See, for example, Washington to Landon Carter, Cambridge, March 25, 1776, *G.W.*, IV, 433-34; Washington to John Augustine Washington, Cambridge, March 31, 1776, *G.W.*, IV, 447-48.

37. General Orders, Cambridge, November 28, 1775, *G.W.*, IV, 119.

38. General Orders, Headquarters, New York, June 30, 1776, *G.W.*, V, 205-6.

39. General Orders, Headquarters, New York, July 2, 1776, *G.W.*, V, 211.

40. General Orders, Headquarters, near Germantown, September 13, 1777, *G.W.*, IX, 211.

41. General Orders, Headquarters, Orangetown, Tuesday, September 26, 1780, *G.W.*, XX, 95.

42. General Orders, Friday, April 18, 1783, *G.W.*, XXVI, 334-35.

43. Washington to the Inhabitants of Princeton and Neighborhood, together with the President and Faculty of the College, Rocky Hill, August 25, 1783, *G.W.*, XXVII, 116.

44. Farewell Orders to the Armies of the United States, Rock Hill, near Princeton, November 2, 1783, *G.W.*, XXVII, 223.

45. *G.W.*, XXVII, 227.

46. Address to Congress on Resigning His Commission [Annapolis, December 23, 1783], *G.W.*, XXVII, 284.

47. William Meade, *Old Churches, Ministers and Families of Virginia* (2 vols.; Philadelphia, 1857), II, 253.

48. Morris, *Christian Life and Character of the Civil Institutions of the United States* (Philadelphia, 1864), pp. 289-90.

49. Douglas Southall Freeman noted that the religious tone of Washington's addresses and circulars became more pronounced after David Humphreys and Jonathan Trumbull, Jr., both theologically-minded New Englanders, joined his staff and began assisting him in the preparation of public papers. "The part these two men played in accentuating and enlarging with their pens the place that Providence had in the mind of Washington was probably among the most extraordinary and least considered influences of puritanism on the thought of the young nation. The people who heard the replies of Washington to their addresses doubtless thought they were listening to the General, as indeed they were, to the extent that Washington did not cancel what had been written; but the warmth of the faith was more definitely that of the aide than that of the Commander-in-Chief." Freeman, *George Washington, A Biography*, V, *Victory with the Help of France* (New York, 1952), 493.

50. Morris, *op. cit.*, p. 290.

51. First Inaugural Address, April 30, 1789, *G.W.*, XXX, 292-93.

52. Proclamation, Philadelphia, January 1, 1795, James D. Richardson, ed., *A Compilation of the Messages and Papers of the Presidents, 1789-1897* (Washington, 1896), I, 180.

53. Thanksgiving Proclamation, City of New York, October 3, 1789, *G.W.*, XXX, 427-28.

54. Anson Phelps Stokes, *Church and State in the United States* (3 vols.; New York, 1950), I, 487.

55. *G.W.*, XXX, 428n.

56. Charles Warren, *Odd Byways in American History* (Cambridge, 1942), p. 222.

57. *Ibid.*, pp. 221-43.

58. Richardson, *op. cit.*, I, 180.

59. See John Adams' proclamation for days of "solemn humiliation, fasting, and prayer" for March 23, 1798, and March 6, 1799, *ibid.*, I, 269-70, 284-86.

CHAPTER IV

1. William Roscoe Thayer, *George Washington* (Boston and New York, 1922), p. 2.

2. William White to Colonel Hugh Mercer, Philadelphia, November

28, 1832, in Bird Wilson, *Memoir of the Life of the Right Reverend William White* (Philadelphia, 1839), p. 190.

3. Samuel Miller, *The Life of Samuel Miller* (2 vols.; Philadelphia, 1869), I, 123.

4. Aaron Bancroft, *An Essay on the Life of George Washington* (Worcester, 1807), p. 530.

5. John Marshall, *The Life of George Washington* (2 vols.; 2d ed.; Philadelphia, 1836), II, 445.

6. Jared Sparks, ed., *The Writings of George Washington* (12 vols.; Boston, 1837), XII, Appendix, "Religious Opinions and Habits of Washington," 399-411; Washington Irving, *Life of George Washington* (8 vols.; New York, 1857), I, 162, 397; II, 362-63; VIII, 123.

7. John E. Remsburg, *The Fathers of Our Republic: Paine, Jefferson, Washington, Franklin, A Lecture Delivered before the Tenth Annual Congress of the American Secular Union, in Chickering Hall, New York, November 13, 1886* (Boston, 1887); Remsburg, *Six Historic Americans* (New York, 1906), pp. 101-45, mainly a rehash of his 1886 and other lectures on Washington's religion.

8. Henry Cabot Lodge, *George Washington* (2 vols.; Boston and New York, 1889); Woodrow Wilson, *George Washington* (New York, 1896); Thayer, *Washington* (1922); Luther A. Weigle, *American Idealism* (New Haven, 1928); John C. Fitzpatrick, "George Washington and Religion," Part I of *Washington as a Religious Man*, Pamphlet Number 5 of the Series, "Honor to George Washington," ed. Albert Bushnell Hart (Washington, D.C.: George Washington Bicentennial Commission, 1931).

9. Rupert Hughes, *George Washington* (3 vols.; New York, 1926-30), I, 552-59; III, 270-98.

10. Douglas Southall Freeman, *George Washington, A Biography* (7 vols.; New York, 1948-57).

11. Speech to the Delaware Chiefs, Headquarters, Middle Brook, May 12, 1779, *G.W.*, XV, 55 and note.

12. To the Chiefs and Warriors, Representatives of the Wyandots, Delawares, Shawnoes, Ottawas, Chippewas, Potawatimes, Miamis, Eel River, Weeas, Kickapoos, Piankashaws, and Kaskaskias [Philadelphia, November 29, 1796], *G.W.*, XXXV, 302 and note.

13. *G.W.*, V, 245.

14. *G.W.*, XI, 342-43.

15. Joseph Buffington, *The Soul of Washington* (Philadelphia, 1936), p. 106.

16. Circular to the States, Headquarters, Newburgh, June 8, 1783, *G.W.*, XXVI, 483-96.

17. *G.W.*, XXVI, 485. "It is hard to read these sentences without agitation and tears," declared social critic Paul Goodman, recently, "for they are simply true and simply patriotic." Paul Goodman, *Growing Up Absurd* (New York, 1960), p. 96.

18. *G.W.*, XXVI, 496.

19. Edward C. McGuire, *The Religious Opinions and Character of Washington* (New York, 1836), p. 72.

20. Buffington, *Soul of Washington,* p. 140.

21. Letter by Lodge in *New York Daily Tribune,* Monday, May 26, 1902.

22. The phrase, "the State over which you preside" was changed to "the United States" and the reference to the soldiers was omitted.

23. For a critical discussion of "Washington's Prayer," see W.H. Whittekin, "George Never So Prayed," *Truth Seeker,* LVI (July 27, 1929), 474; Franklin Steiner, "That Alleged Prayer of G. Washington," *ibid.,* LIV (July 28, 1927), 474-75; Steiner, "That Washington Prayer Again," *ibid.,* LIV (December 31, 1927), 842.

24. *The World Almanac* (New York, 1930), p. 906.

25. Albert R. Beatty, "Was Washington Religious?" *National Republic,* XX (March, 1933), 18.

26. *American Bar Association Journal,* XXXIII (July, 1947), 658.

27. *Truth Seeker,* LIV, 842.

28. Joseph McCabe, "Six Infidel Presidents," *Haldeman-Julius Quarterly* (April, 1927), p. 40.

29. Rupert Hughes, *George Washington, the Savior of the States, 1777-1781* (New York, 1930), p. 291.

30. *Ibid.,* p. 290.

31. Douglas Southall Freeman, *George Washington, A Biography,* Volume V, *Victory with the Help of France* (New York, 1952), 443.

32. Commenting on the part that Jonathan Trumbull, Jr., and David Humphreys played in "accentuating and enlarging with their pens the place that Providence had in the mind of Washington," Freeman declared that "the warmth of the faith" contained in Washington's Revolutionary addresses and circulars was "more definitely that of the aide than that of the Commander-in-Chief." *Ibid.,* p. 493. See chap. iii, note 49.

33. *G.W.,* XXVI, 496n.

34. *G.W.,* I, xliii.

35. *G.W.,* I, xlv.

36. *G.W.,* XI, 483n.

37. To Gouverneur Morris, Valley Forge, May 29, 1778, *G.W.,* XI, 483.

38. James B. Buckley, "Washington as a Christian and a Communicant," *Independent,* L (February 19, 1898), 206.

39. L.H. Butterfield, ed., *Letters of Benjamin Rush* (2 vols.; Princeton, 1951), I, 7, 10-11, 419.

40. Lester J. Capon, ed., *The Adams-Jefferson Letters* (2 vols.; Chapel Hill, 1959), II, 343.

41. Albert Ellery Bergh, ed., *The Writings of Thomas Jefferson* (20 vols.; Washington, D.C., 1904-5), X, 381-85; Thomas Jefferson, *The Jefferson Bible, Being the Life and Morals of Jesus Christ of Nazareth* (Greenwich, Connecticut, 1961).

42. Daniel Edwin Wheeler, ed., *Life and Writings of Thomas Paine* (10 vols.; New York, 1908), VI, 8-9.

43. Washington to Major General Israel Putnam, Camp, 20 Miles from Philadelphia, October 19, 1777, *G.W.,* IX, 401.

44. Washington to John Christian Ehler, Philadelphia, December 23, 1793, *G.W.*, XXXIII, 215.

45. Washington to the Countess of Huntingdon, Mount Vernon, June 30, 1785, *G.W.*, XXVIII, 180-81.

46. Washington to John Ettwin, Mount Vernon, May 2, 1788, *G.W.*, XXIX, 489.

47. *Ibid.* In an address to the Society of the United Brethren for Propagating the Gospel among the Heathen, July 10, 1789, Washington also praised "the disinterested endeavors of your Society to civilize and christianize the Savages of the Wilderness." Papers, CCCXXXIV, 34.

48. Washington to Rev. William White, Mount Vernon, May 30, 1799, *G.W.*, XXXVII, 216-17.

49. Washington to Rev. Nathaniel Whitaker, Valley Forge, December 20, 1777, *G.W.*, X, 175.

50. Washington to Rev. Uzal Ogden, West Point, August 5, 1779, *G.W.*, XVI, 51.

51. John C. Thorne, "A Monograph on the Rev. Israel Evans, Chaplain in the Revolutionary Army," *Magazine of History, with Notes and Queries, Extra Number*, no. 1 (Concord, New Hampshire, 1902; reprinted New York, 1907), pp. 13-14.

52. Washington to Rev. Israel Evans, Headquarters, Valley Forge, March 13, 1778, *G.W.*, XI, 78.

53. William B. Sprague, *Life of Jedidiah Morse* (New York, 1875), 231-32.

54. Washington to Jedidiah Morse, Mount Vernon, February 28, 1799, *G.W.*, XXXVII, 140.

55. Washington to Rev. Zechariah Lewis, Mount Vernon, August 14, 1797, *G.W.*, XXXVI, 7.

56. Benjamin Stevens, *A Sermon Occasioned by the Death of the Honourable Sir William Pepperell* (Boston, 1759).

57. *Ibid.*, p. 2.

58. *Ibid.*, p. 4.

59. *Ibid.*, p. 8.

60. *Ibid.*, p. 11.

61. *Ibid.*, p. 24.

62. Washington to Rev. Joseph Buckmaster, New York, December 23, 1789, *G.W.*, XXX, 484.

63. Samuel Eliot Morison, *The Young Man Washington* (Cambridge, 1932), p. 37.

64. Paul Leicester Ford, ed., *The Works of Thomas Jefferson* (12 vols.; New York and London, 1904), I, 352.

65. See, for example, J. M. Robertson, *A History of Free Thought in the Nineteenth Century* (2 vols.; New York, 1930), I, 53; J.V. Nash, "The Religion and Philosophy of Washington," *Open Court*, XLIII (February, 1932), 73-92.

66. R.H. Sudds, "Benjamin Rush," *Dictionary of American Biography* (22 vols.; New York, 1928-40), VII, 536-37. Interestingly, in "The Belknap Papers" there is a letter to Jeremy Belknap dated November 19, 1790, in

which Rush declares: "George Washington's example is truly excellent. He seems not only to believe the Gospel, but to *feel* its spirit. I wish the same could be said of all the great officers of the government." *Collections of the Massachusetts Historical Society*, Sixth Series, IV (Boston, 1891), 472-73. Rush seems to have changed his mind about Washington by the time he had his conversation with Jefferson.

67. J.H. Jones, *The Life of Ashbel Green* (New York, 1849).

68. Papers, CCCXXXVI, 280-81.

69. *Ibid.*, p. 282.

70. Arthur Bullis Bradford (1819-99) studied at Princeton Seminary, was licensed by the Presbytery of Philadelphia, and between 1837 and 1847 held pastorates in various churches in Pennsylvania and New Jersey. In 1847 he took part in the formation of the Free Presbyterian Church, an antislavery denomination, and served the Free Church of New Castle from 1853 to 1868, with the exception of the year 1862-63, when he was United States Consul at Amoy, under the appointment of President Lincoln. With the dissolution of the Free Presbyterian Church after the Civil War, Bradford, who had "undergone a decided change of theological opinion," was, at his own request, permitted to withdraw from the Presbyterian ministry. He retired to a farm at Enon Valley, Pennsylvania, occupying himself with literary pursuits and occasional lecturing. *Necrological Reports and Annual Proceedings of the Alumni Association of Princeton Theological Seminary*, II, 1890-1899 (Princeton, New Jersey, 1899), 508-9.

71. Undated letter from A.B. Bradford to B.F. Underwood, quoted in John E. Remsburg, *Six Historic Americans*, p. 125. It was presumably written some time after 1868, when Bradford retired from the ministry.

72. *Ibid.*, p. 126.

73. Ashbel Green, "Jefferson's Papers," *Christian Advocate*, VIII (1830), 307.

74. *Ibid.*, p. 308. In a letter to Rev. B.C.C. Parker, Philadelphia, November 28, 1832, Bishop White corroborated Green's statement. It was not "the sense of the body" of clergymen at the time, he declared, "to elicit the opinion of the President on the subject of the Christian religion." Wilson, *op. cit.*, pp. 190-91.

75. *Christian Advocate*, VIII, 308.

76. *Ibid.*

77. *Works of Jefferson*, I, 352-53.

78. *Christian Advocate*, VIII, 308.

79. *Works of Jefferson*, I, 353.

80. *Christian Advocate*, VIII, 308-9.

81. Papers, CCCXXXIV, 28.

82. *Ibid.*, p. 50.

83. *Ibid.*, p. 100.

84. *Treaties, Conventions, International Acts, Protocols and Agreements between the United States of America and Other Powers* (4 vols.; Washington, D.C., 1910-38), II, 1786.

85. Anson Phelps Stokes, *Church and State in the United States* (3 vols.; New York, 1950), I, 498.

86. Charles Swain Hall, *Benjamin Tallmadge, Revolutionary Soldier and American Businessman* (New York, 1943), p. 167.

87. Samuel Miller, *The Life of Samuel Miller* (2 vols.; Philadelphia, 1869), I, 123.

88. William White to Rev. B.C.C. Parker, Philadelphia, December 21, 1832, in Wilson, *op. cit.*, p. 193.

89. "After-Dinner Anecdotes of James Madison, Excerpts from Jared Sparks' Journal for 1829-31," *Virginia Magazine of History and Biography*, LX (April, 1952), 263.

90. Wilson, *op. cit.*, pp. 187-88.

91. James Abercrombie to Origen Bacheler, November 29, 1831, *Magazine of American History*, XIII (June, 1885), 597.

CHAPTER V

1. Washington to Dr. James Anderson, Philadelphia, December 24, 1795, *G.W.*, XXXIV, 407.

2. "The Belknap Papers," *Collections of the Massachusetts Historical Society*, III, Fifth Series (1877), 123.

3. To Rev. William Gordon, New York, May 13, 1776, *G.W.*, XXXVII, 526.

4. To Colonel Thomas McKean, Headquarters, New York, August 13, 1776, *G.W.*, V, 428.

5. Address to Congress, Princeton, August 26, 1783, *G.W.*, XXVII, 117.

6. To James McHenry, Mount Vernon, July 31, 1778, *G.W.*, XXX, 30.

7. To the Massachusetts Assembly, March 28, 1776, *G.W.*, IV, 441-42.

8. To Martha Custis, July 20, 1758, *G.W.*, II, 242.

9. To Major General Israel Putnam, Headquarters, Cambridge, March 29, 1776, *G.W.*, IV, 444.

10. To Dr. Thomas Ruston, Mount Vernon, August 31, 1788, *G.W.*, XXX, 79.

11. To Rev. Jonathan Boucher, Mount Vernon, August 14, 1798, *G.W.*, XXXVI, 414.

12. To James McHenry, Mount Vernon, July 31, 1778, *G.W.*, XXX, 30.

13. To Thomas Nelson, Mount Vernon, August 3, 1788, *G.W.*, XXX, 34.

14. To Dr. James Anderson, Mount Vernon, July 25, 1798, *G.W.*, XXXVI, 365.

15. To Governor Jonathan Trumbull, Cambridge, July 18, 1775, *G.W.*, III, 344.

16. To Bryan Fairfax, Valley Forge, March 1, 1778, *G.W.*, III, 344.

17. To Landon Carter, Cambridge, March 25, 1776; to John Augustine Washington, Cambridge, March 31, 1776, *G.W.*, IV, 433, 447.

18. To the Mayor, Recorder, Aldermen, and Commonalty of New York City, April 10, 1785, *G.W.*, XXVIII, 126.

19. To Marquis de Chastellux, Mount Vernon, September 5, 1785, *G.W.*, XXVIII, 254.

20. To Marquis de Lafayette, Mount Vernon, May 10, 1786, *G.W.*, XXVIII, 421.

21. To Bryan Fairfax, Valley Forge, March 1, 1778, *G.W.*, XI, 3.

22. To William Pearce, Philadelphia, May 25, 1794, *G.W.*, XXXIII, 375.

23. To Governor Jonathan Trumbull, Philadelphia, May 15, 1784, *G.W.*, XXVII, 399.

24. To David Humphreys, Philadelphia, March 23, 1793, *G.W.*, XXXII, 398.

25. To the Mayor, Corporation, and Citizens of Alexandria [Alexandria, April 16, 1789], *G.W.*, XXX, 287.

26. General Orders, Headquarters, Valley Forge, Saturday, May 2, 1778, *G.W.*, XI, 343.

27. To the President of Congress, New York, July 10, 1776, *G.W.*, XI, 247.

28. To Major General Philip Schuyler, Cambridge, January 27, 1776, *G.W.*, IV, 281.

29. To Landon Carter, Valley Forge, May 30, 1778, *G.W.*, XI, 492.

30. To Governor Jonathan Trumbull, Headquarters, September 6, 1778, *G.W.*, XII, 406.

31. To Lund Washington, Morristown, May 19, 1780, *G.W.*, XVIII, 392.

32. To Brigadier General John Sullivan, New York, June 13, 1776, *G.W.*, V, 133.

33. To Joseph Reed, Cambridge, January 4, 1776, *G.W.*, IV, 211-12.

34. To John Adams, New York, April 15, 1776, *G.W.*, IV, 484.

35. To John Smith, William McGuire, Charles Thruston, Robert White, Junior and Hugh Holmes, U.S., November 28, 1796, *G.W.*, XXXV, 294.

36. To John Augustine Washington, Brunswick in New Jersey, July 4, 1778, *G.W.*, XII, 157.

37. To Samuel Bishop, Mayor of New Haven, Connecticut, August 24, 1793, *G.W.*, XXXIII, 59.

38. To Rev. Bryan Fairfax, Philadelphia, March 6, 1793, *G.W.*, XXXII, 376.

39. The First Inaugural Address, April 30, 1789, *G.W.*, XXX, 294.

40. To Joseph Reed, Cambridge, March 7, 1776, *G.W.*, IV, 380.

41. To the Magistrates and Military Officers of Schenectady, Schenectady, June 30, 1782, *G.W.*, XXIV, 390.

42. To Watson and Cassoul, State of New York, August 10, 1782, *G.W.*, XXIV, 497.

43. To John Robinson, Camp at Fort Cumberland, September 1, 1758, *G.W.*, II, 276.

44. To Governor Jonathan Trumbull, Philadelphia, May 15, 1784, *G.W.*, XXVII, 399.

45. To William Pearce, Philadelphia, December 29, 1793, *G.W.*, XXXIII, 218.

46. To David Humphreys, Mount Vernon, February 7, 1785, *G.W.*, XXVIII, 66.

47. To Rev. William Gordon, Headquarters, Newburgh, July 8, 1783, *G.W.*, XXVII, 50.

48. To Philip Schuyler, May 9, 1789, *G.W.*, XXX, 317.

49. To William Tudor, Mount Vernon, August 18, 1788, *G.W.*, XXX, 55.

50. To Annis Boudinot Stockton, Mount Vernon, August 31, 1788, *G.W.*, XXX, 76.

51. To John Quincy Adams, Mount Vernon, January 20, 1799, *G.W.*, XXXVI, 313.

52. To the Earl of Buchan, Philadelphia, May 26, 1794, *G.W.*, XXXIII, 383.

53. To the President of the United States, Mount Vernon, July 4, 1798, *G.W.*, XXXVI, 313.

54. To Thaddeus Kosciuszko, Mount Vernon, August 31, 1797, *G.W.*, XXII, 36.

55. To Burwell Bassett, Mount Vernon, April 25, 1778, *G.W.*, III, 133.

56. To Lund Washington, Headquarters, Middlebrook, May 29, 1779, *G.W.*, XV, 180.

57. To Governor Jonathan Trumbull, New York, August 18, 1776, *G.W.*, V, 453.

58. To the Officers and Soldiers of the Pennsylvania Associators, August 8, 1776, *G.W.*, V, 398.

59. To Brigadier General Samuel Holden Parsons, Morristown, April 23, 1777, *G.W.*, VII, 456.

60. To Brigadier General Thomas Nelson, Camp at White Marsh, 12 miles from Philadelphia, November 8, 1777, *G.W.*, X, 28.

61. To John Armstrong, Headquarters, Middle Brook, May 18, 1779, *G.W.*, XV, 99.

62. To James McHenry, Philadelphia, July 18, 1782, *G.W.*, XXIV, 432.

63. [Proposed Address to Congress, April ? 1789], *G.W.*, XXX, 308.

64. To John Jay (Private), Philadelphia, November 1 (-5), 1794, *G.W.*, XXXIV, 16.

65. To John Augustine Washington, Philadelphia, May 31, 1776, *G.W.*, V, 93.

66. To the Officers and Soldiers of the Pennsylvania Associators, August 6, 1777, *G.W.*, V, 398.

67. To the President of the United States, Mount Vernon, July 13, 1798, *G.W.*, XXXVI, 328-29.

68. To Rev. Jonathan Boucher, Mount Vernon, August 15, 1798, *G.W.*, XXXVI, 413-14.

69. To Governor Jonathan Trumbull, Philadelphia, May 15, 1784, *G.W.*, XXVII, 399.

70. [Proposed Address to Congress, April ? 1789], *G.W.*, XXX, 301.

71. To Rev. Samuel Langdon, New York, September 28, 1789, *G.W.*, XXX, 416.

72. To Josiah Quincy, Cambridge, March 24, 1776, *G.W.*, IV, 422.

73. To Jonathan Williams, Philadelphia, March 2, 1795, *G.W.*, XXXIV, 130.

74. Farewell Orders to the Armies of the United States, Rock Hill, near Princeton, November 2, 1783, *G.W.*, XXVII, 223.

75. To Brigadier General Thomas Nelson, Camp at the White-plains, August 20, 1778, *G.W.*, XII, 343. But, Washington added, "it will be time enough for me to turn preacher, when my present appointment ceases; and therefore, I shall add no more on the Doctrine of Providence." *(Ibid.)*

76. To Sir Edward Newenham, Mount Vernon, August 29, 1788, *G.W.*, XXX, 72.

77. To Marquis de Lafayette, Mount Vernon, June 19, 1788, *G.W.*, XXIX, 526.

78. To Charles Cotesworth Pinckney, Mount Vernon, June 28, 1788, *G.W.*, XXX, 10.

79. To Benjamin Lincoln, Mount Vernon, June 29, 1788, *G.W.*, XXX, 11.

80. To John Armstrong (Private), Philadelphia, March 11, 1792, *G.W.*, XXXII, 2.

81. To Rev. William Gordon, Newport, March 9, 1781, *G.W.*, XXI, 332.

82. To Mrs. Martha Washington, Philadelphia, June 18, 1775, *G.W.*, III, 294.

83. To Landon Carter, Valley Forge, May 30, 1778, *G.W.*, XI, 492.

84. To Joseph Reed, Cambridge, January 14, 1776, *G.W.*, IV, 243.

85. To Charles Pettit, Mount Vernon, August 16, 1788, *G.W.*, XXX, 42.

86. To Major General Henry Knox, Mount Vernon, February 20, 1784, *G.W.*, XXVII, 340-41.

87. To Rev. William Gordon, Mount Vernon, October 15, 1797, *G.W.*, XXXVI, 49.

88. To Samuel Washington, Germantown, near Philadelphia, August 10, 1777, *G.W.*, IX, 39.

89. To Major General Henry Knox, September 12, 1782, *G.W.*, XXV, 150n.

90. To George Augustine Washington, Philadelphia, January 27, 1793, *G.W.*, XXXII, 315-16.

91. To the Secretary of War, Philadelphia, September 8, 1791, *G.W.*, XXXI, 360.

92. To Rev. Bryan Fairfax, Philadelphia, March 6, 1793, *G.W.*, XXXII, 376.

93. To Elizabeth Parke Custis Law, Philadelphia, March 30, 1796, *G.W.*, XXXV, 1.

94. To Archibald Blair, Mount Vernon, June 24, 1799, *G.W.*, XXXVII, 244.

95. To the Secretary of War, Mount Vernon, May 29, 1797, *G.W.*, XXXV, 456.

96. John Alexander Carroll and Mary Wells Ashworth, *George Washington*, Volume VII, *First in Peace* (New York, 1957), 487.

97. To Colonel Burgess Ball, Mount Vernon, September 22, 1799, *G.W.*, XXXVII, 372.

98. To Henry Knox, Mount Vernon, January 10, 1788, *G.W.*, XXIX, 378.

99. To Jonathan Trumbull, Jr., Mount Vernon, January 5, 1784, *G.W.*, XXVII, 294.

100. To Annis Boudinot Stockton, Mount Vernon, August 31, 1788, *G.W.*, XXX, 76.

101. To Elizabeth Washington Lewis, New York, September 13, 1789, *G.W.*, XXX, 399.

102. To the Secretary of War, Mount Vernon, March 25, 1799, *G.W.*, XXXVII, 158.

103. To Brigadier General Thomas Nelson, Camp at the White-plains, August 20, 1778, *G.W.*, XII, 343.

104. Daniel Edwin Wheeler, ed., *Life and Writings of Thomas Paine* (10 vols.; New York, 1908), VI, 2; Albert Henry Smith, ed., *The Writings of Benjamin Franklin* (10 vols.; New York, 1907), X, 84; Albert Ellery Bergh, ed., *The Writings of Thomas Jefferson*, XVII, v.

105. Tobias Lear, *Letters and Recollections of George Washington* (New York, 1906), p. 133.

106. M. L. Weems, *The Life of George Washington* (29th ed.; Frankford near Philadelphia, 1826), p. 170.

107. Lear, *op. cit.*, pp. 134-35.

108. To Henry Knox, Philadelphia, March 2, 1797; to George Lewis, Mount Vernon, April 9, 1797, *G.W.*, XXXV, 409, 434.

109. Moncure D. Conway, "The Religion of George Washington," *Open Court*, III (October 24, 1889), 1897.

110. To Bryan Lord Fairfax, Mount Vernon, January 20, 1799, *G.W.*, XXXVII, 94-95.

111. *Open Court*, III, 1897.

CHAPTER VI

1. *New York Times*, Monday, October 13, 1958, p. 18.

2. Papers, CCCXXXIV, 84.

3. Washington to Robert Sinclair, Philadelphia, May 6, 1792, *G.W.*, XXXII, 37.

4. *G.W.*, XXVI, 335-36.

5. To Members of the Volunteer Association and Other Inhabitants of the Kingdom of Ireland Who Have Lately Arrived in the City of New York, New York, December 2, 1783, *G.W.*, XXVII, 254.

6. Washington to Tench Tilghman, Mount Vernon, March 24, 1784, *G.W.*, XXVII, 367.

7. Washington to Rev. Francis Adrian Van der Kemp, Mount Vernon, May 28, 1788, *G.W.*, XXIX, 504.

8. William Spohn Baker, *Character Portraits of Washington* (Philadelphia, 1887), p. 77.

9. Joseph Martin Dawson, *Baptists and the American Republic* (Nashville, 1956), p. 90.

10. Gaillard Hunt, *The Life of James Madison* (New York, 1902), p. 12.

11. Jared Sparks, ed., *The Writings of George Washington* (12 vols.; Boston, 1837), II, 481.

12. Washington to Henry Riddell, Mount Vernon, February 22, 1774, *G.W.*, III, 190.

13. Washington to Marquis de Lafayette, Philadelphia, August 15, 1787, *G.W.*, XXIX, 259.

14. Washington to Sir Edward Newenham, Philadelphia, October 20, 1792, *G.W.*, XXXII, 190.

15. Washington to George Mason, Mount Vernon, October 3, 1785, *G.W.*, XXVIII, 285.

16. *G.W.*, XXX, 299.

17. Jefferson to Colonel William Duane, Monticello, July 25, 1811, in Albert Ellery Bergh, ed., *The Writings of Thomas Jefferson* (20 vols.; Washington, D.C., 1904-5), XIII, 67; Jefferson to P. H. Wendover, Monticello, March 13, 1815, *ibid.*, XIV, 279.

18. Washington to Joseph Hopkinson, Mount Vernon, May 27, 1798, *G.W.*, XXXVI, 274.

19. Washington to Thomas Nelson, Mount Vernon, August 3, 1788, *G.W.*, XXX, 34.

20. John C. Fitzpatrick, *George Washington Himself* (Indianapolis, 1933), p. 182.

21. Instructions to Colonel Benedict Arnold, Camp at Cambridge, September 14, 1775, *G.W.*, III, 495-96.

22. Washington to Colonel Benedict Arnold, Camp at Cambridge, September 14, 1775, *G.W.*, III, 492.

23. Robert C. Hartnett, "The Religion of the Founding Fathers," in F. Ernest Johnson, ed., *Wellsprings of the American Spirit* (New York, 1948), p. 53.

24. Rupert Hughes, *George Washington* (3 vols.; New York, 1926-30), II, 343.

25. General Orders, Headquarters, Cambridge, November 5, 1775, *G.W.*, IV, 65.

26. Peter Guilday, *The Life and Times of John Carroll* (2 vols.; New York, 1922), I, 83.

27. Peter Guilday, in foreword to *Eulogy on George Washington Delivered in St. Peter's Church, Baltimore, February 22, 1800, by John Carroll, First Bishop and Archbishop of Baltimore* (New York, 1931), p. xi.

28. John Gilmary Shea, *History of the Catholic Church in the United States* (4 vols.; New York, 1886-92), II, 147.

29. Martin I. J. Griffin, *Catholics and the American Revolution* (3 vols.; Ridley Park, Pennsylvania, 1907-11), I, 213.

30. James Haltigan, *The Irish in the American Revolution* (Washington, D.C., 1908), p. 348.

31. Ray Allen Billington, *The Protestant Crusade, 1800-1860* (New York, 1938), p. 19.

32. *The Life of the Rev. John Murray, Preacher of Universal Salvation, Written by Himself. With a Continuation, by Mrs. Judith Sargent Murray*

(with an introduction and notes by Rev. G. L. Demarest; Boston, 1869), p. 317.

33. General Orders, Headquarters, Cambridge, September 17, 1775, *G.W.*, III, 497.

34. *Life of John Murray*, pp. 316-17.

35. John Prince, quoted by Clarence R. Skinner and Alfred S. Cole, *Hell's Ramparts Fell, the Life of John Murray* (Boston, 1941), p. 125.

36. Richard Eddy, *Universalism in America* (2 vols.; Boston, 1884-86), I, 332.

37. Washington to President of Congress, Headquarters, Middle Brook, June 8, 1777, *G.W.*, VIII, 203-4.

38. Washington to Robert Dinwiddie, Winchester, June 25, 1756, *G.W.*, I, 394.

39. Dinwiddie to Washington, July 1, 1756, *G.W.*, I, 394n.

40. Washington to Robert Dinwiddie, Winchester, August 4, 1756, *G.W.*, I, 420.

41. Dinwiddie to Washington, August 19, 1756, *G.W.*, I, 420n.

42. Washington to Dinwiddie, Winchester, September 8, 1756, *G.W.*, I, 462.

43. Eliphalet Nott Potter, *Washington, A Model in His Library and Life* (New York, 1895), p. 157.

44. Katherine Smyth, "Quaker Contacts with Washington," *Friends Intelligencer*, LXXXIX (February 20, 1932), 144.

45. Moses Brown to William Wilson, Providence, 1st Mo. 2nd, 1776, *Pennsylvania Magazine of History and Biography*, I (1877), 169.

46. Mack E. Thompson, "Moses Brown's 'Account of Journey to Distribute Donations 12th Month 1775,'" *Rhode Island History*, XV (October, 1956), 113.

47. *Pennsylvania Magazine of History and Biography*, I, 170.

48. *Rhode Island History*, XV, 113.

49. George Washington Greene, *The Life of Nathanael Greene* (2 vols.; New York, 1867), I, 142-43.

50. *Rhode Island History*, XV, 113.

51. Augustine Jone, *Moses Brown: His Life and Services* (Providence, 1892), p. 35.

52. To the Pennsylvania Council of Safety, Headquarters, Morristown, January 19, 1777 and January 29, 1777, *G.W.*, VII, 35, 79.

53. Washington to Governor William Livingston, Headquarters, Morristown, May 11, 1777, *G.W.*, VIII, 44-45.

54. Washington to Colonel John Siegfried, Philadelphia County, October 6, 1777, *G.W.*, IX, 318; Powers to Officers to Collect Clothing, etc., Headquarters, November, 1777, *G.W.*, X, 124.

55. MS Minutes of Meetings for Sufferings, Philadelphia Yearly Meeting, Department of Records, 302 Arch Street, Philadelphia, II, 140.

56. Washington to Brigadier General John Lacey, Junior, Headquarters, Valley Forge, March 20, 1778, *G.W.*, XI, 114.

57. "Memoirs of James Pemberton," *Friends' Miscellany*, VII (1835), 65.

58. See James Bowden, *The History of the Society of Friends in America* (3 vols.; London, 1850-54), II, 319-21; Isaac Sharpless, *A History of Quaker Government in Pennsylvania, 1682-1783,* (Philadelphia, 1902), II, 168-69; Margaret E. Hirst, *The Quakers in Peace and War* (London, 1923), p. 396.

59. For a detailed account, see Thomas Gilpin, *Exiles in Virginia* (Philadelphia, 1848).

60. MS Minutes of Philadelphia Yearly Meeting, II, 382-84.

61. *Ibid.,* II, 415.

62. St. John de Crèvecoeur, *Lettres d'un Cultivateur Américain* (3 vols.; Paris, 1787), I, 213. The English version does not contain the passage on Warner Mifflin.

63. General John Armstrong to President Thomas Wharton, October 8, 1777, *Pennsylvania Magazine of History and Biography,* I, 392n.

64. MS Minutes of Philadelphia Yearly Meeting, II, 415.

65. *The Friend of Peace,* II (January, 1820), 8.

66. *Pennsylvania Magazine of History and Biography,* I, 393n.

67. MS Minutes of Philadelphia Yearly Meeting, II, 415.

68. Sharpless, *op. cit.,* II, 169.

69. To President Thomas Wharton, Junior, Headquarters, April 5, 1778, *G.W.,* XI, 221.

70. Henry D. Biddle, ed., *Extracts from the Journal of Elizabeth Drinker* (Philadelphia, 1889), p. 93.

71. To President Thomas Wharton, Junior, Headquarters, Valley Forge, April 6, 1778, *G.W.,* XI, 224.

72. Carl Leopold Baurmeister, *Revolution in America: Confidential Letters and Journals, 1776-1784* (New Brunswick, 1957), p. 168; Gilpin, *op. cit.,* p. 45; Sharpless, *op. cit.,* II, 167-69; Hirst, *op. cit.,* pp. 408-9.

73. Gilpin, *op. cit.,* p. 232.

74. Sharpless, *op. cit.,* II, 168.

75. Rufus M. Jones, *The Quakers in the American Colonies* (London, 1923), p. 260.

76. Sharpless, *op. cit.,* II, 169, 220.

77. Brissot de Warville, *New Travels in the United States of America, Performed in 1788* (New York, 1792), pp. 415-16.

78. *The Friend of Peace,* II, 8.

79. Papers, CCX (November 7-22, 1782).

80. *Autobiography of Charles Biddle, Vice-President of the Supreme Executive Council of Pennsylvania, 1745-1821* (Philadelphia, 1883), pp. 285-86.

81. Papers, CCCXXXIV, 81.

82. *Ibid.,* p. 49.

83. *Ibid.,* CCCXXXV, 13.

84. *Ibid.,* CCCXXXIV, 41.

85. Robert B. C. Howell, *The Early Baptists of Virginia* (Philadelphia, 1857), pp. 224-26.

86. Papers, CCCXXXIV, 82.

87. Conrad Henry Moehlman, *The Wall of Separation between Church and State* (Boston, 1951), p. 87.

88. Albert Henry Newman, *A History of the Baptist Churches in the United States* (New York, 1894), p. 374; Richard B. Cook, *The Story of the Baptists in All Ages and Countries* (Baltimore, 1884), pp. 249-50.

89. Thomas Armitage, *A History of the Baptists* (New York, 1890), p. 806; Benjamin Franklin Riley, *A History of the Baptists in the Southern States East of the Mississippi* (Philadelphia, 1898), p. 106.

90. Madison to Washington, Orange, November 20, 1789, in Gaillard Hunt, ed., *The Writings of James Madison* (9 vols.; New York, 1900-1910), V, 429.

91. Hirst, *op. cit.*, p. 144.

92. Papers, CCCXXXIV, 52.

93. Susanna Dilwyn to her father, 11 mo. 4, 1789, *Friends Intelligencer*, CVI (1949), 700.

94. "Quakers d'Amérique," *Patriote Français*, January 8, 1790.

95. Charles M. Woodman, *Quakers Find a Way* (Indianapolis, 1950), p. 244; Sharpless, *op. cit.*, p. 223.

96. Isaac A. Cornelison, *The Relation of Religion to Civil Government in the United States of America* (New York, 1895), p. 204; Philip Schaff, *Church and State in the United States* (New York, 1888), p. 38n.

97. Jonathan Elliot, ed., *The Debates in the Several State Conventions on the Adoption of the Federal Constitution* (5 vols.; Philadelphia, 1881), I, 385-86.

98. Papers, CCCXXXIV, 77-79.

99. For Washington's associations with the Presbyterians, see Paul F. Boller, Jr., "George Washington and the Presbyterians," *Journal of the Presbyterian Historical Society*, XXXIX (September, 1961), 129-49.

100. Oscar Straus, *Religious Liberty in the United States* (New York, 1896), p. 6.

101. Elliot, *op. cit.*, IV, 195-96.

102. *Gazette of the United States*, Wednesday, May 6, to Saturday, May 9, 1789.

103. *Ibid.*, Wednesday, June 10, 1789.

104. Papers, CCCXXXIV, 97-99.

105. Guilday, *John Carroll*, I, 364.

106. Thomas O'Gorman, *A History of the Roman Catholic Church in the United States* (New York, 1916), p. 273.

107. Guilday, *John Carroll*, I, 367.

108. *Ibid.*

109. Rufus Learsi, *The Jews in America: A History* (Cleveland and New York, 1954), p. 29.

110. Oscar Handlin, *Adventure in Freedom: Three Hundred Years of Jewish Life in America* (New York, 1954), pp. 3-21.

111. "Items Relating to Correspondence of Jews with George Washington," *Publications of the American Jewish Historical Society*, XXVII (1920), 217-22.

112. Moses Seixas to K.K.S.I., Newport, July 2, 1790, *ibid.*, p. 219.

113. Papers, CCCXXXIV, 129-30.

114. Learsi, *op. cit.*, p. 47.

115. Trustees of K.K.S.I. to Newport Congregation, New York, June 20, 1790, *PAJHS*, XXVII (1920), 218.

116. *Ibid.*, 217.

117. Moses Seixas to K.K.S.I., Newport, July 2, 1790, *PAJHS*, XXVII (1920), 219.

118. *Ibid.*

119. Leon Huhner, "The Jews of South Carolina from the Earliest Settlement to the End of the American Revolution," *PAJHS*, XII (1904), 61n.

120. David de Sola Pool, *An Old Faith in the New World, Portrait of Shearith Israel, 1654-1954* (New York, 1955), p. 323.

121. Papers, CCCXXXV, 17-18.

122. Harry Simonhoff, *Jewish Notables in America, 1776-1865* (New York, 1956), p. 73.

123. Pool, *op. cit.*, p. 284.

124. *For the Honor of the Nation, Patriotism of the American Jews Hailed by Christian Historians* (New York, 1939), p. 109.

125. Morris A. Gutstein, *To Bigotry No Sanction, A Jewish Shrine in America, 1658-1958* (New York, 1958), p. 88.

126. Morris A. Gutstein, *The Story of the Jews of Newport* (New York, 1936), p. 212.

127. Pool, *op. cit.*, p. 494.

128. Harry L. Golden and Martin Rywell, *Jews in American History* (Charlotte, 1950), p. 4.

129. Simonhoff, *op. cit.*, p. 76.

130. Golden and Rywell, *op. cit.*, p. 4.

131. Benjamin H. Hartogensis, "Rhode Island and Consanguineous Jewish Marriages," *PAJHS*, XX (1911), 144.

132. Papers, CCCXXXV, 30-31.

133. Morris U. Schappes, ed., *A Documentary History of the Jews of the United States, 1654-1875* (New York, 1950), p. 77.

134. Lee M. Friedman, *Jewish Pioneers and Patriots* (Philadelphia, 1942), p. 21.

135. Max J. Kohler, "As to the Supposed 18th Century Translation into Hebrew of Washington's Correspondence with Hebrew Congregations," *PAJHS*, XXXII (1931), 121.

136. Lee M. Friedman, *Pilgrims in a New Land* (Philadelphia, 1948), p. 134.

137. Pool, *op. cit.*, p. 324; Lee J. Levinger, *A History of the Jews in the United States* (Cincinnati, 1930), p. 125; Tina Levitan, *The Firsts of American Jewish History, 1492-1951* (Brooklyn, 1952, 1957), p. 32.

138. Gutstein, *Jews of Newport*, p. 206.

139. Peter Wiernik, *History of the Jews in America* (New York, 1931), p. 100.

140. E. Milton Altfeld, *The Jews' Struggle for Religious and Civil Liberty in Maryland* (Baltimore, 1924), p. 176.

141. *The Two Hundred and Fiftieth Anniversary of the Settlement of Jews in the United States: Addresses Delivered in Carnegie Hall, New York, on Thanksgiving Day, 1905* (New York, 1906).

142. Leon Huhner, *The Jews of Newport: Address Delivered on the Occasion of Unveiling the Memorial Tablet in the Old Jewish Synagogue at Newport, Rhode Island, September 7, 1908.*

143. Gutstein, *To Bigotry No Sanction*, pp. 140-41.

144. *"To Bigotry No Sanction," A Documented Analysis of Anti-Semitic Propaganda, Prepared by the American Jewish Committee* (1941).

145. Learsi, *op. cit.*, pp. 45-46.

146. Gutstein, *To Bigotry No Sanction*, p. 151.

147. Marguerite Beck Block, *The New Church in the New World* (New York, 1932), p. 87.

148. Robert Hindmarsh, *Rise and Progress of the New Jerusalem Church* (London, 1861), p. 154.

149. Papers, CCCXXXV, 110.

150. Hindmarsh, *op. cit.*, p. 154.

151. *G.W.*, XXXV, 55-56.

152. Marguerite Fellows Melcher, *The Shaker Adventure* (Princeton, 1941), p. 117.

SELECTED BIBLIOGRAPHY

ABRAHAM, LEWIS. "Correspondence between Washington and Jewish Citizens," *Proceedings of the American Jewish Historical Society,* III (1894), 87-96.

BACHELER, ORIGEN and OWEN, ROBERT DALE. *Discussion on the Existence of God and the Authenticity of the Bible.* London, 1840.

BAKER, WILLIAM SPOHN. *Character Portraits of Washington.* Philadelphia, 1887.

BARNES, LEMUEL C. "George Washington and Freedom of Conscience," *Journal of Religion,* XII (October, 1932), 493-525.

————. "The John Gano Evidence of George Washington's Religion," *Bulletin of William Jewell College,* Series No. 24 (September 15, 1926), No. 1.

BEATTY, ALBERT R. "Washington's Christmases," *National Republic,* XX (January, 1933), 3-5, 26.

————. "Was Washington Religious?" *National Republic,* XX (February and March, 1933), 3-5, 28; 18-19, 29.

BOGARD, BEN M. *President Washington a Baptist.* Little Rock, Arkansas (1921?).

BOLLER, PAUL F., JR. "George Washington and the Methodists," *Historical Magazine of the Protestant Episcopal Church,* XXVII (June, 1959), 165-86.

————. "George Washington and the Presbyterians," *Journal of the Presbyterian Historical Society,* XXXIX (September, 1961), 129-49.

————. "George Washington and the Quakers," *Bulletin of Friends Historical Association,* XLIX (Autumn, 1960), 67-83.

BRINKER, EVVA. "George Washington the Vestryman and His Services as a Churchman," *Picket Post* (April, 1948), 14-16.

BRUCE, PHILIP A. *Institutional History of Virginia in the Seventeenth Century.* 2 vols. New York, 1910.

BRYAN, WILLIAM ALFRED. *George Washington in American Literature, 1775-1865.* New York, 1952.

BUCKLEY, JAMES M. "Washington as a Christian and a Communicant," *Independent,* L (February 17 and 24, 1898), 205-7; 240-41.

BUFFINGTON, JOSEPH. *An Overlooked Side of Washington: Being the Bi-Centennial Address Made on Washington's Birthday, 1932, at Valley Forge Memorial Chapel.* Philadelphia, 1932.

————. *The Soul of Washington.* Philadelphia, 1936.

BURK, W. HERBERT. *Washington's Prayers.* Norristown, Pennsylvania, 1907.

————. *The Washington Window in the Washington Memorial Chapel, Valley Forge.* Norristown, Pennsylvania, 1926.

CARROLL, H. K. *The Religious Forces of the United States.* New York, 1912.

CARROLL, JOHN. *Eulogy on George Washington Delivered in St. Peter's Church, Baltimore, February 22, 1800.* New York, 1931.

CATHCART, WILLIAM. *The Baptists and the American Revolution.* Philadelphia, 1876.

COBB, SANFORD H. *The Rise of Religious Liberty in America.* New York, 1902.

CONRAD, FREDERICK W. "Washington: Christianity and the Moulding Power of His Character," *Lutheran Quarterly,* XXVI (1896), 89-115.

CONWAY, MONCURE D. "The Religion of George Washington," *Open Court,* III (October 24, 1889).

DAWSON, JOSEPH MARTIN. *Baptists and the American Republic.* Nashville, 1956.

DEMAREST, WILLIAM H. S. "George Washington's Religion," *Huguenot* (May, 1932), 1, 12.

DORCHESTER, DANIEL. *Christianity in the United States from the First Settlement down to the Present Time.* New York, 1890.

DUNLAP, EDWARD SLATER. *George Washington as a Christian and Churchman.* Washington, D.C., 1932.

EDDY, RICHARD. *Universalism in America: A History.* 2 vols. Boston, 1886.

FITZPATRICK, JOHN C. (ed.). *The Diaries of George Washington, 1748-1799.* 4 vols. Boston, 1925.

_____. *George Washington Himself.* Indianapolis, 1933.

_____. *The Spirit of the Revolution.* Boston, 1924.

_____. *Washington as a Religious Man,* Pamphlet No. 5 of the series "Honor to George Washington," edited by Dr. Albert Bushnell Hart. Washington, D.C.: George Washington Bicentennial Commission, 1931.

_____. *The Writings of George Washington.* 39 vols. Washington, D.C., 1931-44.

FORD, PAUL LEICESTER. *The True George Washington.* Philadelphia, 1896.

FREEMAN, DOUGLAS SOUTHALL. *George Washington, A Biography.* 7 vols. (Vol. 7, *First in Peace,* by John Alexander Carroll and Mary Wells Ashworth.) New York, 1948-57.

FRIEDMAN, LEE M. *Jewish Pioneers and Patriots.* Philadelphia, 1942.

———. *Pilgrims in a New Land.* Philadelphia, 1948.

GILLETT, E. H. *History of the Presbyterian Church in the United States of America.* 2 vols. Philadelphia, 1864.

GOODMAN, ABRAM V. *American Overture, Jewish Rights in Colonial Times.* Philadelphia, 1947.

GOODWIN, EDWARD L. *The Colonial Church in Virginia.* Milwaukee, 1927.

GREELY, A. W. "The Personal Side of Washington's Domestic and Religious Life," *Ladies' Home Journal,* XIII (April, 1896).

GREEN, ASHBEL. "Jefferson's Papers," *Christian Advocate,* VIII (1830), 305-10.

———. *The Life of Ashbel Green.* New York, 1849.

GREENE, E. B. *The Revolutionary Generation, 1763-1790.* New York, 1943.

GRISWOLD, RUFUS W. *The Republican Court, or American Society in the Days of Washington.* New York, 1855.

GUILDAY, PETER. *The Life and Times of John Carroll.* New York, 1922.

HALL, THOMAS C. *The Religious Background of American Culture.* Boston, 1930.

HALLGREN, MAURITZ. *Landscape of Freedom: The Story of American Liberty and Bigotry.* New York, 1941.

HANDLIN, OSCAR. *Adventure in Freedom.* New York, 1954.

HARRIS, CARLTON D. "Was Washington a Christian or Profane, Irreligious and Worldly-Minded?" *Minute Man,* XXI (June, 1926), 83-87.

HEADLEY, J. T. *The Chaplains and Clergy of the American Revolution.* New York, 1864.

HINDMARSH, ROBERT. *The Rise and Progress of the New Jerusalem Church.* London, 1861.

HOSACK, DAVID. *Memoir of DeWitt Clinton.* New York, 1829.

HOWELL, ROBERT B. C. *The Early Baptists of Virginia.* Philadelphia, 1857.

HUGHES, RUPERT. *George Washington.* 3 vols. New York, 1926-30.

HUHNER, LEON. "The Jews of Virginia from the Earliest Times to the Close of the Eighteenth Century," *Publications of the American Jewish Historical Society,* XX (1911), 85-105.

HUMPHREY, EDWARD FRANK. *Nationalism and Religion in America, 1774-1789.* Boston, 1924.

HUMPHREYS, FRANK LANDON. *George Washington, the Churchman.* N.p., 1932.

IRVING, WASHINGTON. *Life of George Washington.* 8 vols. New York, 1857.

"Items Relating to Correspondence of Jews with George Washington," *Publications of the American Jewish Historical Society,* XXVII (1920), 217-22.

JAMES, CHARLES F. *Documentary History of the Struggle for Religious Liberty in Virginia.* Lynchburg, 1900.

JOHNSON, ALVIN and YOST, FRANK H. *Separation of Church and State in the United States.* Minneapolis, 1948.

JOHNSON, F. ERNEST (ed.). *Wellsprings of the American Spirit.* New York, 1948.

JOHNSTONE, WILLIAM J. *George Washington the Christian.* Cincinnati, 1919.

———. *How Washington Prayed.* New York, 1932.

KINSOLVING, ARTHUR B. "The Religion of George Washington," *Historical Magazine of the Protestant Episcopal Church,* XVIII (September, 1949), 326-32.

KIRKLAND, CAROLINE M. *Memoirs of Washington*. New York, 1857.

KOCH, ADOLF G. *Republican Religion: The American Revolution and the Cult of Reason*. New York, 1933.

KREMER, A. H. "The Religious Character of Washington," *Mercersburg Review*, XI (1859), 211-22.

LEAR, TOBIAS. *Letters and Recollections of George Washington*. New York, 1906.

LEVITAN, TINA. *The Firsts of American Jewish History, 1492-1951*. Brooklyn, 1952, 1957.

LODGE, HENRY CABOT. *George Washington*. 2 vols. Boston, 1889.

McCABE, JOSEPH. "Six Infidel Presidents," *Haldeman-Julius Quarterly* (April, 1927), 37-40.

McCOMAS, JOSEPH PATTON. "Washington — the Churchman in New York," *Huguenot* (February, 1932), 4, 9, 12.

McGUIRE, EDWARD C. *The Religious Opinions and Character of Washington*. New York, 1836.

MANROSS, WILLIAM W. *A History of the American Episcopal Church*. New York, 1950.

MARCUS, JACOB R. *Early American Jewry, the Jews of New York, New England, and Canada, 1649-1794*. 2 vols. Philadelphia, 1951.

MARSHALL, JOHN. *The Life of George Washington*. 2 vols. 2nd ed. Philadelphia, 1836.

MAYNARD, THEODORE. *The Story of American Catholicism*. New York, 1941.

MEADE, WILLIAM. *Old Churches, Ministers and Families of Virginia*. 2 vols. Philadelphia, 1857.

Memoirs of Washington, by His Adopted Son, George Washington Parke Custis, with a Memoir of the Author, by his

Daughter; and Illustrative and Explanatory Notes by Benson J. Lossing. New York, 1859.

MILLER, J. LEROY. "Where Washington Prayed Thousands Now Will Pray," *American Magazine*, CVIII (August, 1929).

MOEHLMAN, CONRAD HENRY. *The Wall of Separation between Church and State.* Boston, 1951.

MORAIS, HERBERT M. *Deism in Eighteenth Century America.* London, 1934.

MORISON, SAMUEL ELIOT. *The Young Man Washington.* Cambridge, 1932.

MORRIS, B. F. *Christian Life and Character of the Civil Institutions of the United States.* Philadelphia, 1864.

NASH, J. V. "The Religion and Philosophy of Washington," *Open Court*, XLIII (February, 1932), 73-92.

O'GORMAN, THOMAS. *A History of the Roman Catholic Church in the United States.* New York, 1916.

OLDHAM, G. ASHTON. "Washington, Christian Statesman," *Homiletic Review*, XCV (February, 1928), 144-46.

PALTSITS, VICTOR HUGO. *Washington's Farewell Address.* New York, 1935.

POOL, DAVID DE SOLA and TAMAR. *An Old Faith in the New World, Portrait of Shearith Israel, 1654-1954.* New York, 1955.

PORTER, FRANK G. "Washington as Bishop Asbury Saw Him; the View of a Contemporary," *Methodist Review*, CXIII (July, 1930), 513-21.

POTTER, ELIPHALET NOTT. *Washington, A Model in His Library and Life.* New York, 1895.

REMSBURG, JOHN E. *Six Historic Americans.* New York, 1906.

ROBERTSON, JOHN M. *A History of Free Thought in the Nineteenth Century.* New York, 1930.

SCHAPPES, MORRIS U. (ed.) *A Documentary History of the Jews of the United States, 1654-1875.* New York, 1950.

SEARS, LOUIS M. *George Washington.* New York, 1932.

SLAUGHTER, PHILIP. *Christianity the Key to the Character and Career of Washington: A Discourse Delivered before the Ladies of the Mt. Vernon Association of the Union, at Pohick Church, Truro Parish, Virginia, on the Thirtieth Day of May, 1886.* Washington, D.C., 1886.

————. *The History of Truro Parish in Virginia.* Philadelphia, 1908.

SPARKS, JARED (ed.). *The Writings of George Washington.* 12 vols. Boston, 1837.

SPRAGUE, WILLIAM B. *Annals of the American Pulpit.* 9 vols. New York, 1859-69.

STEINER, FRANKLIN. "That Alleged Prayer of G. Washington," *Truth Seeker,* LIV (July 28, 1927), 474-75.

————. "That Washington Prayer Again," *Truth Seeker,* LIX (December 31, 1927), 842.

STEPHENSON, NATHANIEL W. and DUNN, WALDO H. *George Washington.* New York, 1940.

STOKES, ANSON PHELPS. *Church and State in the United States.* 3 vols. New York, 1950.

STONE, WILLIAM L. "Was Washington a Christian," *Magazine of American History,* XIII (June, 1885), 596-97.

TAYLOR, MALCOLM. "Washington as a Christian," *Magazine of History,* XXII (1915), 88-93.

THOM, WILLIAM T. *The Struggle for Religious Freedom in Virginia: The Baptists.* Johns Hopkins University Studies in History and Political Science. Baltimore, 1900.

ULMANN, ALBERT. "George Washington and the Jews," *Judaean Addresses,* IV (1933), 202-11.

VERNON, MERLE. *Washington: The Soldier and the Christian.* New York, n.d.

"Washington as a Communicant of the Church, Testimony of an Eye-Witness to Washington's Frequent Communions while President," *Churchman,* LXXIX (1899), 795-98.

"Washington at Morristown during the Winter of 1779-80," *Harper's New Monthly Magazine,* XVIII (February, 1859), 289-309.

"Washington at the Communion Table in Morristown, New Jersey," *Presbyterian Magazine,* I (December, 1851), 569-71.

WATSON, JOHN F. *Annals and Occurrences of New York City and State.* Philadelphia, 1846.

————. *Annals of Philadelphia and Pennsylvania, in the Olden Time.* 3 vols. Philadelphia, 1881.

WEEMS, MASON LOCKE. *The Life of George Washington.* 29th ed. Frankford near Philadelphia, 1826.

WHITTEKIN, W. H. "George Never So Prayed," *Truth Seeker,* LVI (July 27, 1929), 474.

WILSON, BIRD. *Memoir of the Life of the Right Reverend William White.* Philadelphia, 1839.

WOODWARD, WILLIAM E. *George Washington, the Image and the Man.* New York, 1926.

WYLIE, T. W. J. *Washington, a Christian: A Discourse Preached February 23, 1862, in the First Reformed Presbyterian Church, Philadelphia.* Philadelphia, 1862.

INDEX

229